Beginner's Guide Samsung Galaxy Note 20 and Note 20 Ultra

Hidden Tips and Tricks to Operate Your New Samsung Galaxy Note 20 Series Like a Pro

Nobert Young

TABLE OF CONTENT

Introduction

Congratulations on purchasing the latest addition to the Samsung family, the Note 20 series. Now, you need a well-illustrated user guide that contains all the hidden tips and tricks to help you to maximize the full potentials of your Samsung Note 20. This user guide contains all the hidden tricks and tips that you need to know to familiarize yourself with the powerful Samsung Note 20 and Note 20 Ultra.

The Galaxy Note 20 series is a powerful flagship phone that comes with several new features, some of which are not yet available in any other smartphone brand in the world today. You have the advanced cameras, smooth 120Hz display, 50X zoom, and other amazing features packed in a compact design.

There is a whole lot to know about these new Samsung devices.

Let's get started.

Chapter 1: Getting Started/ Unboxing Samsung Note 20

SIM Installation

Install SIM/microSD card
Place the SIM card and optional microSD card (sold separately) into the tray with the gold contacts facing down.

Charge your device
Before turning on your device, charge it fully.

Set up the Samsung Galaxy Note 20 Series
Follow the steps below to set up your new device:

- Insert your SIM card into the SIM tray before you power on your phone.
- Select your language at the "Let's go" screen, then click on the blue arrow to begin the process of setting up your new phone

- Read the terms and conditions, tick the box beside '**I have read and agree to all of the above.**' Click on **Next.**

- Follow the instructions on your screen to restore your content from an old device or click on '**Skip this for Now.**'

- Click on **Next.**

- Select your Wi-fi network. You may be required to input your password. Then tap **Next.**

- Sign in to your Google account with your existing details or create a new account, then click on **Next** to proceed.

- Review Google's terms of service and click on "**I agree**" to proceed.

- To restore your previously saved backups, follow the instructions on your screen or click on **'Don't Restore.'**
- Your device will then prompt you to set up your fingerprints, facial recognition, password or PIN. You may skip this stage for now.

- Read through the Google services page, toggle on the options you need then click on **'Accept.'**

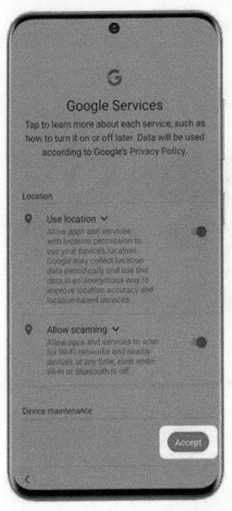

- Read and choose additional apps you want to download and install during the initial set up. Click on **OK.**

- Create your Samsung account or log in with your existing details.

- Review and agree to the presented terms and conditions, then click on **Next.**

- Restore your saved data from Samsung Cloud or click on **Skip.**

- Click **Finish** once done and begin to use your new phone.

Power On Your Device

To power on your device,

- Press and hold down on the side key until the screen lights up.

Switch Off Your Device

To turn the phone off,

- Pull down the Notification panel from the top of your screen.

- Click on **Power**

- Then click on **Power Off**

- Confirm your action when prompted

Here's another way to turn off your device

- Press the Volume down and side keys at the same time.

Restart Your Device

- Pull down the Notification panel from the top of your screen.

- Click on **Power**

- Then click on **Restart**

Auto- Restart Your Device

You can set your device to auto-restart at a specified time.

- Go to Settings.

- Tap **Device Care**

- Click on the 3-dot icon at the right top corner of your screen.

- Then select **Auto Restart**

- Choose your scheduled time and date

- Enable the feature before you exit the menu.

With this option enabled, your phone will automatically restart once a week at the specified time and date. This will help your phone to run smoother and better.

Transfer Data From an Old Device
You can use Smart Switch to move videos, messages, calendars, notes, photos, contacts, and more from your old device to the Note 20.

To do this,

- Go to Settings.

- Click on **Accounts and Backup.**

- Then click on **Smart Switch.**

- Follow the prompts on your screen and select the contents you want to move

Note: Ensure that your battery is fully charged before attempting this as it may drain your battery fast.

Double Tap to Wake Up
The display feature of the Galaxy Note 20 shows you a preview of the battery percentage, notifications, as well as the time and date. You can also use face unlock or ultrasonic fingerprint scanner to wake the phone. But, the 'double-tap to wake' feature is more helpful when you need to wake your screen with just the power key. Enable this feature with the steps below:

- Go to Settings.

- Click on **Advanced Features.**
- Click on **Motion and Gestures.**
- Now toggle on the **Double Tap to Wake Up** option.

Lift to Wake Feature

This feature, once enabled, allows you to unlock your phone just by staring into the phone. Bring the phone close to your face, and the device will scan your eyes to confirm ownership before unlocking the phone. This is particularly useful to persons that unlock their phone via biometric options like the iris sensor or intelligent scan.

- Go to Settings.
- Click on **Advanced Features.**
- Tap **Motions and Gestures.**
- Then toggle on the switch for **Lift to Wake.**

Force-close Apps

There are times when an app will hang & affect the performance of your phone. In times like this, follow the steps below to force-close apps:

- Click on the app switcher button to display all your recently used apps.
- Then swipe up on the preview of an app to force-close the app.
- To close all the apps at the same time, tap the **Close All** button at the bottom of the screen.

Status Icons

Battery full

Battery low

Charging

Mute

Vibrate

Airplane mode

Bluetooth active

Wi-Fi active

Location active

Alarm

Notification icons

Missed calls

Call in progress

Call on hold

New message

Voicemail

New email

Download

Upload

Wi-Fi available

App update

Set Up Samsung Backup

When you first set up your phone, you will receive a prompt to sign in to your Samsung account to be able to perform functions like download apps from the Galaxy store or set up Samsung Pay. Apart from this, it also allows you to enjoy Samsung's backup service. Your device will be routinely backed up so that you can quickly restore things like installed apps, or even the home screen layout of a previous Samsung device with just a few taps. Follow the steps below to check that the Samsung backup is enabled:

- Go to **Settings.**
- Click on **Accounts and Backup.**
- Tap **Samsung Cloud.**

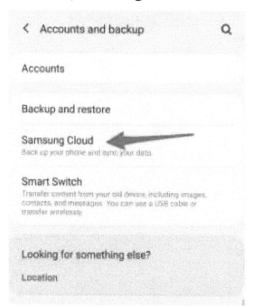

- Click on the 3-dot icon ⋮ at the right top corner of your device.
- Click on **Settings.**
- Select the first option **Sync and Auto-Backup Settings.**

- Go through the list on the next screen to confirm that all you
  need to back up is included in the list.

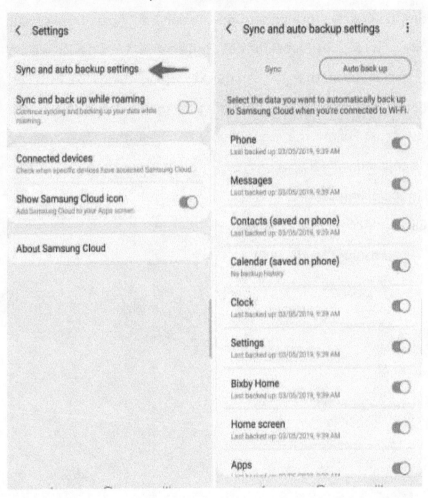

Chapter 2: Side Key Settings

Let's explore how to customize the shortcuts assigned to the Note 20 side key.

Double Press
To choose what happens when you press the side key twice

- Go to Settings.

- Click on **Advanced Features** ✿.

- Then click on **Side Key.**

- Click on **Double Press** to enable the feature then choose from the displayed option:

  1. Open app 2. Open Bixby 3. Quick launch camera (default)

Press and Hold
To choose what happens when you press and hold the side key,

- Go to Settings.

- Click on **Advanced Features** ✿.

- Then click on **Side Key.**

- Click on **Press and Hold** to enable the option, then choose from the displayed option

  1. Power off menu 2. Wake Bixby (default)

Chapter 3: S Pen

The S Pen on the Galaxy Note 20 is just like a real pen, only that it does more than what a real pen can do. You can use the S Pen to write on your phone as well as use it as a wireless controller for your phone. In this chapter, we will look at the things that you can do with the S Pen.

Activate the S Pen as a Remote
The S Pen can do lots of things, including taking photos from a distance, controlling your PowerPoint presentations and so on. But first, you need to activate the S Pen to serve as a remote.

- Go to Settings.

- Click on **Advanced Features**

- Select **S Pen,** then tap **Air Action.**

- Move the switch at the top of your screen to the right to enable the remote feature.

Screen-Off Memos
This feature allows you to take notes on your Samsung Galaxy without unlocking your phone screen. Here are two ways that you can access the screen-off memos on your phone

- With your phone screen off, pull out the S Pen & begin writing.

- If you already have the S Pen out, hold down the S pen button, then click on your phone's screen while it is off to activate screen off memo.

- To add pages to your note, click the down arrow.

- Tap **Save** once done, and your writing will be stored in the Notes app on your phone.

Disable Screen Off Memo

The 'Screen Off Memo' feature is activated by default. However, you can disable it and turn it on later.

- Go to Settings.

- Click on **Advanced Features**

- Click on **S Pen,** click on **Screen Off Memo** and move the switch to the left to disable the feature.

Annotate PDFs

You can import PDF files on your phone and annotate them without installing another app.

- Open the document in Samsung Notes, then pull out your S Pen or tap the side button to write, save and share the document with your contact or receivers.

Write on Calendar

The Write on Calendar feature of your phone makes it very easy for you to coordinate your schedules. This shortcut launches your calendar to the current month and allows you to add notes as well as share your calendar.

- Pull out the S Pen or click on the side button to launch the Air Command menu.
- Choose **Write on Calendar** to open your calendar to the current month.
- Add notes, block out dates and other editings, then tap **Save.**

Here is another way to access **Write on Calendar**

- Open the Calendar app, then hit the pen icon at the top right side of the app to sync your schedules.

Convert Your Handwriting

After writing with the S Pen, you can convert the handwritten words to text, then save it as a word document or paste it into an email.

- Open the Samsung Notes app and click on .
- Click on icon at the top of your screen.

Enter text using the keyboard.

Write or draw with pens.

Paint with brushes.

Save

Insert files.

- Pull out your S Pen and begin to write. Once done, tap the words with your finger. Click on to select all the handwritten words on the current page.

- Click on **Convert** in the preview window to turn the handwritten words into text.

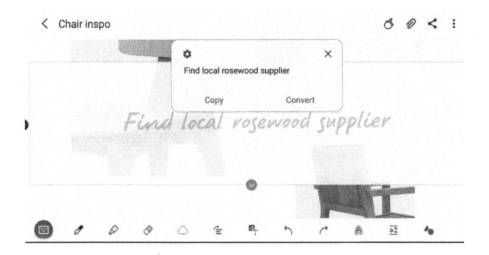

< Chair inspo

Find local rosewood supplier

Copy   Convert

Find local rosewood supplier

- Click on **Save.**
- Click on the Share icon located at the top right side of your screen, then select the media type: **Image, PDF, Text.**

Smart Select

You can use the S Pen to clip, select and collect information that is displayed on your phone screen to share immediately or at a later time. Here is how to use it.

- Pull out the S Pen or press the Pen button to launch the Air Command menu.
- Click on the **Smart Select** icon, then use your Pen to draw a square or a box around the content that you want to copy and save.

- Click on the **Collect** icon at the bottom right side of your screen.

- The screenshot will save as a floating square at the top right side of your screen.

- To share, click the thumbnail, then select a sharing option from the list on your screen: **Share Via** or **Save in Scrapbook.**

- To delete the thumbnail, press down on the floating square until a trash can icon appears at the top of your page. Tap the icon to delete the image.

Activate S Pen Alarm Feature

Due to the size of the S Pen, it is easy to misplace it. However, with this feature enabled, your phone will beep when you begin to walk away from the S Pen.

- Go to Settings.

- Click on **Advanced Features**

- Click on **S Pen.**

- Toggle on **Pen Proximity Alert** under the **Removal** section.

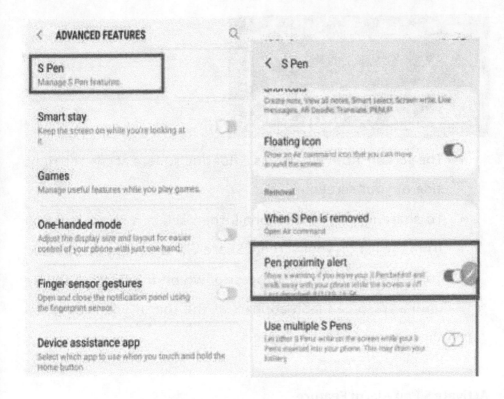

Take Photos Using the S Pen

You can place your phone in a distance and use the S Pen to control the camera.

- Take out the S Pen, then launch your phone camera.
- Set your phone away from you and ensure that the subject is nicely fitted in the camera frame.
- Press the S Pen button once to take a photo.

Switch to Different Camera Mode Using the S Pen

You can use the S Pen to move from the Photo mode to any other mode.

- Take out the S Pen, then launch your phone camera.

- With the S Pen pointing at your phone screen, move it to the right and to the left to get to your desired camera mode.

Switch to Rear or Front Camera Using the S Pen

If your phone camera is set to the rear lens, this is how to switch to the selfie camera and vice versa using the S Pen.

- Take out the S Pen, then launch your phone camera.
- With the S Pen pointing at your phone screen, move the S Pen up and down to go from the rear camera to the front camera and back.

Zoom Using the S Pen

To zoom in or out while in the camera app,

- Navigate to the Photo mode and rotate the pen to zoom in or out.

Customize Air Actions

You can customize the S Pen to determine what should happen when you use the pen as a wand or when you tap the pen button.

- Take the S Pen out of its holder to activate the Air Command option.
- Click the icon by the bottom left side of your screen.
- Tap **Air Action,** then click on **Hold Down Pen Button To.** Assign a feature or an app to the Hold Down Pen Button option.
- Tap the back button to go to the previous screen. Under **App Actions,** click on individual apps to launch the settings.

- On the next screen, under **Gestures,** choose the function that should happen when you move the Pen **Up, Down, Left** & **Right**.

- Under **Pen Button,** choose what should happen when you press the S Pen button once as well as when you press the button two times.

- Under **General App Actions,** click on the individual options and modify as you like.

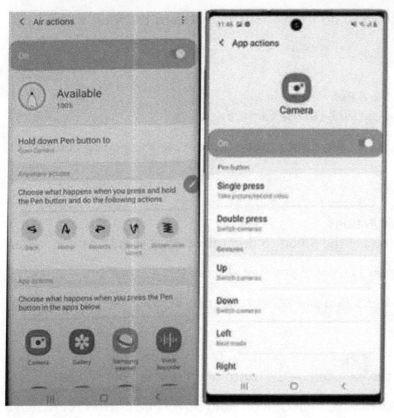

Pair More S Pen

Follow the steps below to pair more than one S Pen with your smartphone.

- Go to Settings.

- Click on **Advanced Features** ⚙️.

- Select **S Pen,** then move the switch beside **Allow Multiple S-Pen** to the right to enable the feature.

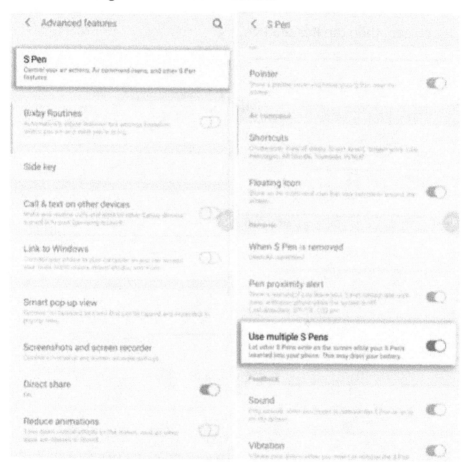

Reset Your S Pen

Peradventure you experience any issue using the S Pen, resetting the pen will take care of these problems like a connection problem, speed and so on.

- Go to Settings.

- Click on **Advanced Features** ⚙.

- Select **S Pen,** then tap **Air Actions.**

- Tap the 3-dot ⋮ menu at the top right side of your phone screen, then tap **Reset S Pen.**

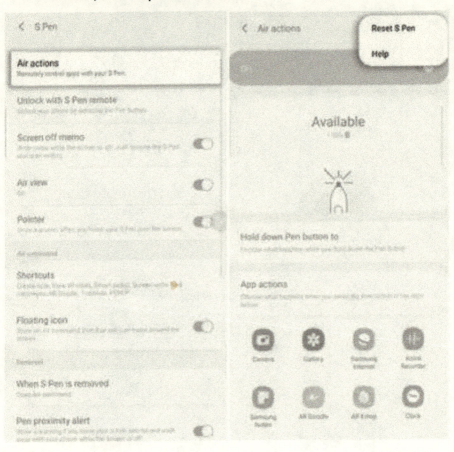

Chapter 4: Key Settings to Activate

Transfer Files Instantly with Quick Share

If you receive and share photos and files frequently, you may want to enable the **Quick Share feature.** This feature allows you to share files to other tablets and phones quickly via Wi-fi direct. Now, let's look at how to set up Quick Share

- Pull down the notification bar & long-press on **Quick Share** icon.
- Now select who should be able to share files with you: **Everyone** or **Contacts only**

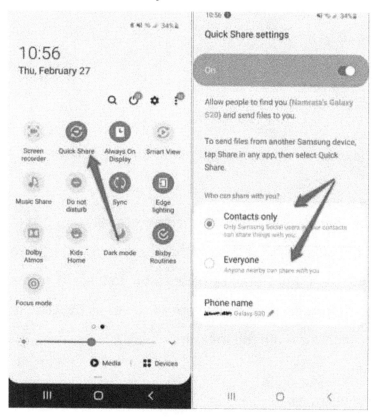

- Now, edit your phone name for easy recognition.

- Go to the sender's phone, pull down the Quick Settings bar and click on the Phone Visibility icon to activate it.
- Once enabled, the compatible phones will pop up on the sharing screen.

- Click on the one you want to complete the sharing in seconds.

Set Up and Use Music Share

This feature allows your friends and family members to play music from their phones via your Bluetooth speakers without connecting directly to your Bluetooth speakers. Both phones have to be connected to the same Wi-fi for this feature to work. Your Note 20 serves as the conduit for connecting their phones with the speakers.

- Go to Settings.
- Click on **Connections.**
- Select **Bluetooth.**

- Then click on **Advanced.**

- Now toggle on the option for **Music Share.**

- Click on **Music Share** to customize sharing options

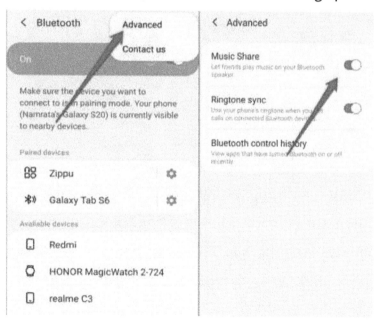

- On the next screen, set the option for **'Share Devices With'** to **Contacts only** so that only persons on your contact list can access the feature.

- Click on **'Ask for Permission to Connect'** and choose your preference from the available options: **Don't ask** or **Every time.**

- The option **"Disconnect When Nothing Is Played For"** is used to deactivate your Bluetooth devices when not in use. Choose from the displayed option as suits your preference.

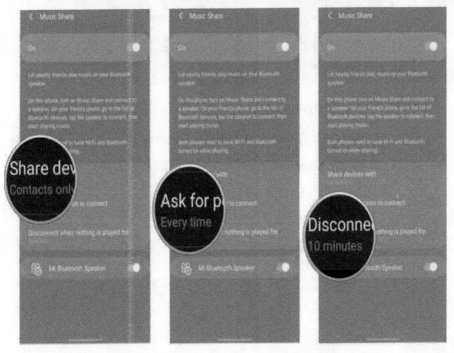

- Now that you have set up the Music Share, proceed to connect your Note 20 to a Bluetooth speaker in your home.

- Your phone will then show on the Bluetooth speaker list of your contacts, and they can connect directly and begin playing.

Enable Nearby Share

Quickly share documents, files, music, etc. with other nearby phones. Note that you can only share with someone that is on your contact list. This is how to enable and set up **Nearby Share**

- Swipe down to the bottom of your screen to go to the Notification panel.
- Click on **Nearby Sharing** or long-press the icon to enter the Setting mode.
- Move the switch beside **Nearby Share** to the right to enable it, then click on **Device Visibility** and select your preferred sharing option.
- After you have enabled the option, open the content that you want to share, then tap the Share icon.
- Click on the receiver, then point your Samsung Note 20 towards the receiver's phone.
- Click on the contact to start the sharing process. As soon as the receiver **Accepts** the transfer, the file will begin to move from you to the receiver.

Customize Quick Share Settings

Apart from choosing the people that can receive from you, you can also select the people that should be able to send to you.

- Open the content that you want to share, then tap the Share icon.

- Tap **Quick Share** at the top of your screen, then tap 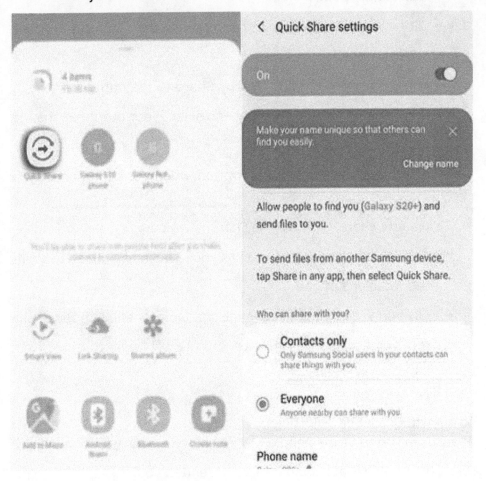 by the top right side of your phone screen.

- On the next screen, you can change your phone name, enable or disable quick share as well as choose the persons that can share with you.

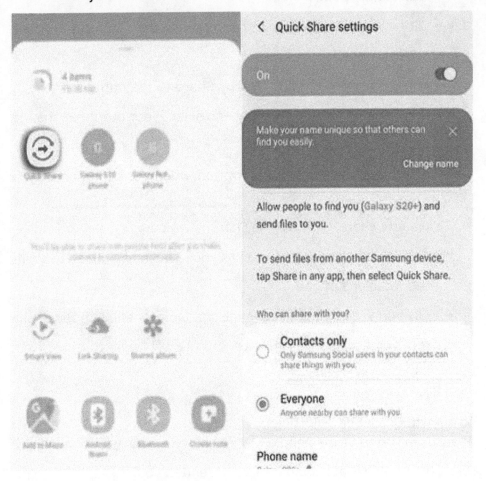

Attend to Calls from Your Connected Devices

With this feature, you can connect your Samsung phones with your tablets so that if you do not have your NOTE 20 with you at any time, you can still use the tablet to receive your text and calls from the Galaxy NOTE 20. Ensure to sign in using your Samsung details on all the devices you want to connect or link. To enable this feature,

- Go to Settings.

- Click on **Advanced Features**

- Move the switch beside **Call & Text on Other Devices** to the right to enable the function. Click on **Agree.**

- Do the steps above on the Samsung Galaxy Note 20 and the other Samsung device that you want to pair.

- After you successfully enable the feature on the two devices, Samsung will automatically complete the process. When next you receive a call, both phones will ring, and you can choose to pick on the second device.

- To quickly enable or disable this feature swipe down to the bottom of your screen then tap on **Call and Text on Other Devices** to enable or disable.

Remove Registered Device

You can link up to three devices using the **Call & Text on Other Devices** feature. You can always remove a registered device at any time using the steps below.

- On your Note 20, open the Settings app and tap **Advanced Features.**

- Tap **Call & Text on Other Devices** then click the 3-dot ⋮ menu at the top side of your phone screen.

- Select **Remove Device,** then choose the device you want to delete. Tap **Remove** to confirm your action.

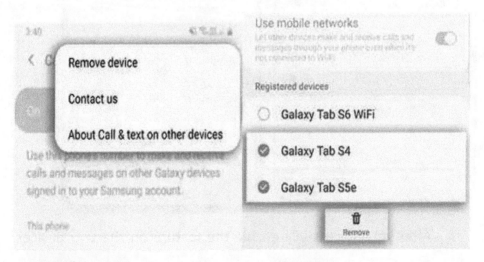

Link Your Phone to Your Computer

This action will enable you to send out messages directly from your computer or even transfer photos from your phone to your computer. But, you will need to log in using your Microsoft account on your phone and computer to be able to use this feature. To enable this link,

- Go to settings
- Click on **Advanced Features.**
- Toggle on the **Link to Windows** option, and your phone will walk you through the remaining setup.
- Easy and fast.

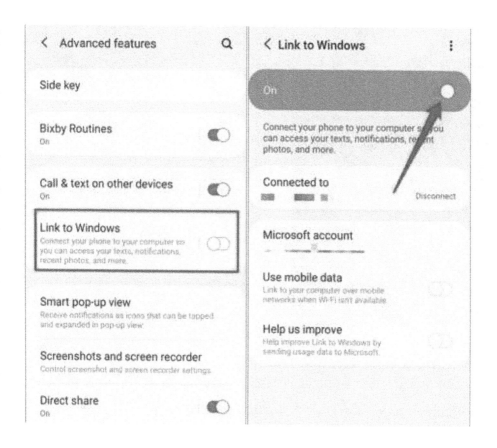

Get Rid of the App Tray or Customize it

By default, swiping up from the bottom of your screen will launch the app tray. However, you can choose to have all your apps on your home screen without any app screen.

- Swipe up to access the app tray. Tap the three-dot ⋮ menu at the top of your screen.

- Click on **Home Screen Settings.**

- To get rid of the app drawer, click on **Home Screen Layout.**

- Then set the option to **Home Screen Only.**

Power and Volume Keys Shortcut

You can quickly access the accessibility settings of your phone by using the volume and power keys. To activate this feature

- Go to Settings.

- Click on **Accessibility.**

- Select **Advanced Settings.**

- Click on **Power and Volume Up Keys.**

- Now toggle on the feature. Then toggle on the options that you want to access when you quickly press the volume up and power keys.

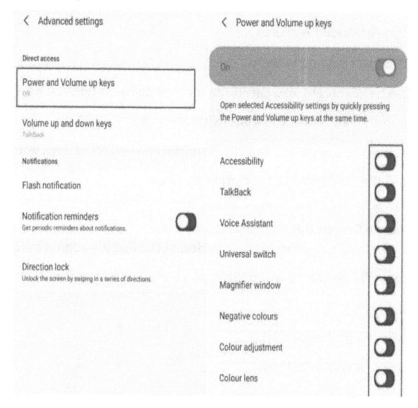

Show Battery Percentage in the Status Bar

By default, you cannot view the battery percentage on the status bar, but you can turn it on from your phone settings. To activate this option,

- Go to Settings.

- Click on **Notifications.**

- Tap **Status Bar.**

- Then toggle on the switch for **Show Battery Percentage**

Get Pop-up Chat Heads for your Messaging App
You can set your device to display chat heads like the one used by the Facebook messenger when using any messaging app.

- Go to Settings.

- Click on **Advanced features**

- Select **Smart pop-up view**

- On the next screen, you can disable or enable pop-up alerts for any app that supports the multi-window mode.

- When next you receive a notification from the selected app, you can tap the chat head to read and respond.

Move the Google Search Bar to the Bottom
Do you know that you can change the position of the Google search bar? This bar is typically placed in the middle of your screen by default. To achieve this,

- Long-press on the search bar.

- Then drag it to the bottom.

- Now, you can just click on it and begin to type your search term without fear of stretching your finger or your phone falling.

Enable Caller ID and Spam Protection

Spam calls can be a nuisance, but the good news is that the Note 20 has a spam protection service integrated into the dialer to prevent spam calls from getting in. To enable this feature,

- Open the dialer from your home screen.

- Click on the 3-dot ⋮ icon on the right.

- Select **Settings**

- Toggle on **Caller ID and Spam Protection.**
- Review the privacy policy and check the boxes.
- Click on **Agree** to accept and finish.

Enable Digital Wellbeing

This feature helps you to monitor the amount of time you spend using your mobile device. By monitoring and tracking your phone usage, it displays a visual representation of your phone habits like the number of times you unlocked your phone, screen time, etc. To access this,

- Go to Settings.

- Select **Digital Wellbeing** from the displayed list.

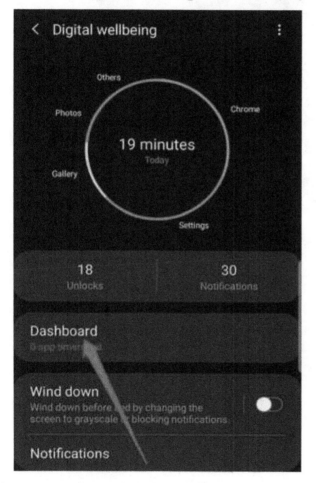

Also, you can set timers for certain apps through the Dashboard option

- Navigate to the desired app on this screen

- Click on the **'No Timer'** dropdown button
- Select your choice from the displayed list

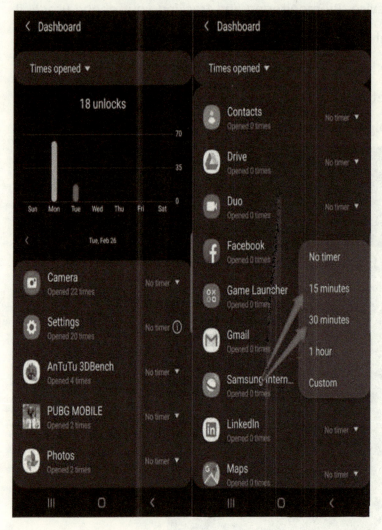

Chapter 5: Taking Screenshots on the Galaxy Note 20

During the day, you may have reasons to capture your screen and save or share the screenshots with others. Now, you have more than one way you can take a screenshot of your screen.

Screenshot Using a Key Combination

With the removal of the Bixby button and the power button turning into a multi-purpose button, it may seem difficult using the buttons. Find below how you can take a screenshot using the key combination

- Open the content you want to screenshot
- Now press the volume down and power button at the same time for one second. Then release both buttons.
- You will see the screen flash.
- And your screenshot is ready.
- You can share the screenshot by clicking on the bottom bar that appears on your screen (far right button), or you can view the screenshot from the notification shade.
- You can also use the center button to enter the editing mode. This mode lets you draw and crop the screenshot before saving or sharing.

Swipe Palm to Take Screenshot

This a great alternative to the usual way of taking screenshots. This feature allows you to take a screenshot by swiping the edge of your hand across your screen. To activate the feature,

- Go to Settings.

- Click on **Advanced Features.**

- Click on **Motion and Gestures.**

- Now toggle on the option for **Palm Swipe to Capture.**

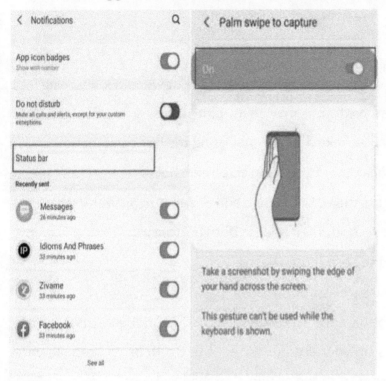

After you have enabled the swipe palm feature, now follow the steps below to capture your screen.

- Open the content you want to screenshot.

- Position your hand vertically on the right or left edge of your phone, then swipe it across the screen in one motion. Ensure to keep your hand in contact with your phone screen while doing this.

- You will now see the screen flash to confirm that the screenshot is complete.

- You can edit, share, or save the screenshot from the notification shade or directly from the on-screen toolbar.

Screenshot Using Bixby Voice
Another way to screenshot your screen is via Bixby Voice.

- Open the content you want to screenshot
- If you configured voice control, say **"Hey Bixby"** or if you have set up your phone's side button for Bixby, press and hold down the side button. A long-press of the button will automatically launch Bixby voice after you must have opened it once.
- With Bixby voice open, say, **"take a screenshot."**
- The screenshot will save in your gallery, where you can share, edit or view it.

Capture More with Scroll Capture
Regardless of the way you take the screenshot, a set of options will appear at the bottom of your screen after capturing. One of these options is called **Screen Capture.** This button is located on the left side of your screen, represented by a box that has down-facing arrows in it. This feature makes the phone to scroll through the content you have on your screen and take several screenshots. All the screenshots will then be joined together to give one complete screenshot of the whole captured content. This is particularly useful for capturing a long restaurant menu, a full webpage, or a set of multiple directions. Just click on the scroll capture button as many times as needed to capture

the full content. It will automatically stop once you get to the bottom of your screen. You can also save, share, or edit the screenshots.

If you do not want to keep tapping, just hold down on the scrolling button to capture a whole page or document in one swoop.

To view the screenshot, go to your gallery app. All screenshots are saved in the screenshot album and also in the main camera roll.

Chapter 6: Maximize Battery Life of your Phone

In this chapter, we will discuss ways to make your battery last longer. Whenever you have a low battery, and need the battery to take you for a little longer, follow any of the steps below to save more battery life.

Switch to FHD Display

Your Samsung Note 20 allows you to switch between WQHD+ and FHD+ screen resolutions. While the former looks amazing with its sharper images and vibrant colors, the latter is best for daily usage.

- Go to settings.
- Click on **Display.**
- Click on **Screen Resolution**.
- Then click on FHD+ and Tap **Apply** to confirm.
- You can always switch to QHD+ whenever you want to watch a TV show or a movie.

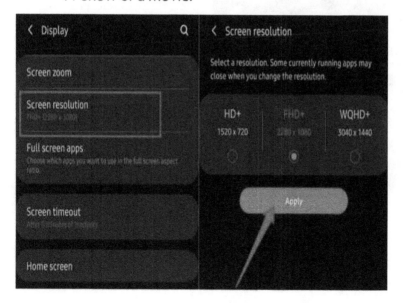

Activate Night Mode

One important thing you should do once you get your phone is to enable Night mode. This feature will switch your phone to dark mode and help to preserve battery life. When the phone is on night mode, the entire screen goes black, as opposed to the light mode that turns on most of the pixels and drains your battery faster. To enable night mode

- Go to Settings.
- Click on **Display.**
- Then toggle the switch for Night mode.

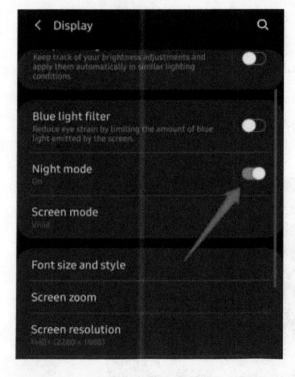

Disable Always on Display

No doubt, the Always On Display (AOD) screen looks very cool, but it also drains the battery faster. So, if you need your phone battery to last a little longer, you may switch off **Always on Display** from the Quick Settings menu.

However, the best way to use the Always-on Display option is to set it on schedule. For instance, if you do not need the Always-on Display screen during a certain period of the day, you can schedule the timing.

- Go to **Settings.**
- Click on the **Lock screen.**
- Click on **Always On Display.**
- Tap **Display Mode.**

- Click on the third option and select your choice.

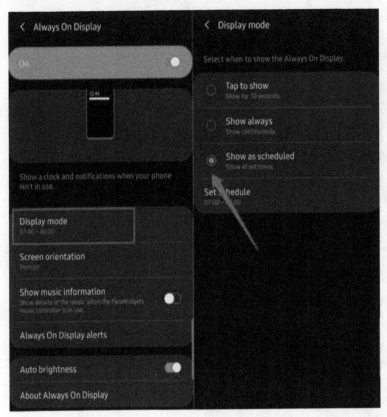

- Alternatively, click on **Tap to show.** This option will display the necessary options whenever you tap on your screen. But will return to the usual mode after ten seconds of inactivity.

Tip: when the Auto brightness setting for AOD is activated, it will automatically adjust the AOD brightness in terms of ambient brightness

Adaptive Battery

This feature, introduced in the S10 series, uses machine language to study your phone habits and app usage. With this, it can disable any app that drains the device battery unnecessarily. To enable this option,

- Go to **Settings.**

- Click on **Device care.**

- Click on **Battery.**

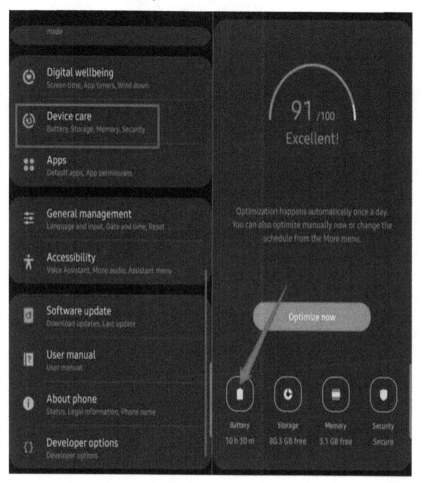

- Click on **Power Mode.**

- Then toggle the switch beside **"Adaptive Power Saving"** to the right to enable the feature. The feature does not begin work immediately as it first needs to learn your phone habits.

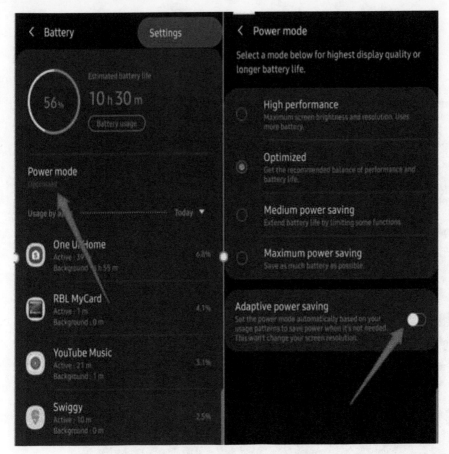

To see how your phone classifies apps, first enable the Developer options. To enable developer options,

- Go to Settings.
- Click on **About phone.**
- Tap **Software Information.**
- Then click on **Build number** 7 times.
- Once the developer option is enabled, you can now search for standby apps.

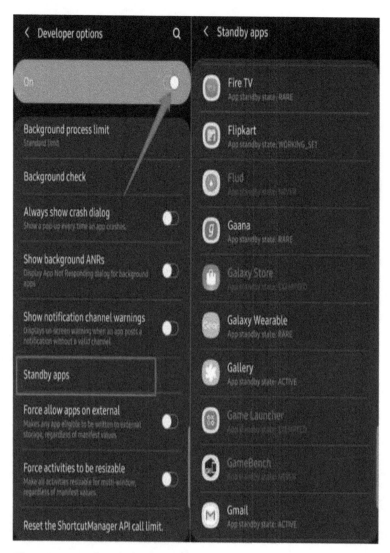

The Note 20 by default, categories apps into the categories below:

- Frequent

- Active

- Rare

- Working set

- Never

To manually change the categories, click on an app, and choose the option that you think is best for the app.

Enable Fast Charging
- Go to **Settings.**
- Click on **Device Care.**
- Tap **Battery.**
- Click on the 3-dot ⋮ icon at the top right side of your screen.
- Select **Settings.**
- Then enable the option for fast charging, if disabled.

Power Modes
You can also check the power modes while on the battery page. The Note 20 series comes with three modes: Medium power-saving, High performance, and Maximum power saving modes. The default setting is optimized to suit your needs, but to get the best from your battery, you may enable one of the modes.

- Go to **Settings.**
- Click on **Device care.**
- Tap **Battery.**
- Click on **Power Mode.**
- Then select your preferred choice

Optimize Settings

The battery optimization of the Note 20 series activates when you are not using your device. This feature automatically reduces screen time timeout, screen brightness, and media volume. To activate this feature,

- Go to **Settings.**
- Click on **Device care.**
- Tap **Battery.**
- Then click on the three-dot ⋮ menu at the right top side of your screen.
- Click on **Settings.**
- Then search for **Optimize settings** and toggle on the switch to activate it.

- You may also enable the options for **Adaptive Battery** and **'Put Unused Apps to Sleep.'**

Reduce Screen Timeout

Another way to save your battery is to check out the Screen timeout settings. If you are fond of dropping your phone without locking it, it will help your device battery and security if you activate screen-on time. The advisable screen-on time is 30 seconds.

To activate this change,

- Go to Settings.

- Click on **Display.**

- Click on **Screen Timeout.**

- Now select your preferred time

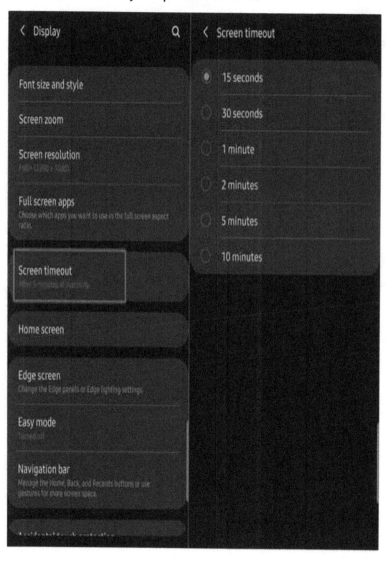

Wireless PowerShare

You can use your Galaxy Note 20 to charge another device wirelessly. The feature responsible for this is called the Wireless PowerShare. Follow the steps below to activate this feature

- Open the quick settings panel (swipe down to the bottom of your screen).
- Click on **Wireless PoweShare** to turn it on.
- Then place the second device on the center of your Note 20, with their backs facing to begin charging

Note: Ensure that your NOTE 20 has over 30% battery life remaining before you use this feature.

Smartphone	Galaxy Watch	Galaxy Buds

Chapter 7: Customize the Home Screen and Lock Screen

The Home screen and lock screen are two screens we use the most on our phones. Thanks to the Android customization options, we can now customize these screens to suit our purposes. So here are tips for the Note 20 home screen and lock screen.

Display Icons in the Lock Screen
Would you want your device to display all your notifications on your lock screen? Maybe not. Thankfully, the Note 20 has the option for you to hide your notifications. You can customize it to display only the notification icons or a brief message, just like you have on the AOD screen. This way, you get to know what the notification is about while hiding the full content. Follow the steps below to make these changes:

- Go to Settings.
- Click on **Lock Screen.**
- Select **Notifications.**
- Then click on **View Style.**
- Select **Icons Only.**

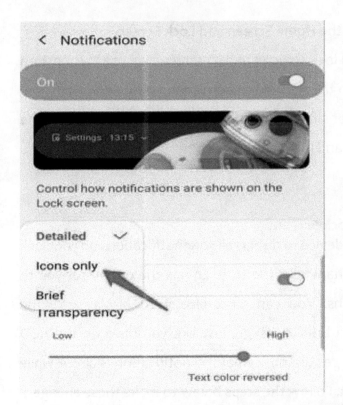

But, if you really want to see all your notifications on the lock screen, you can set the notification box to be transparent by dragging the **Transparency** bar to the right.

Discover New Sets of Clock Faces

Using the current clock faces of the Samsung devices can get boring. Thankfully, Samsung's ClockFace app has lots of stylish clock faces. Plus, you can choose your preferred color. Sadly, this is not available globally, but you can get the APK file from APK Mirror, download the file and enjoy the feature. After you must have installed the Clockface app,

- Go to Settings.

- Click on **Lock Screen.**

- Select **Clock Style.**

- Click on **Always-on Display.**

- Scroll to the left end of your screen and click on the clock icon to display all the new clock faces.

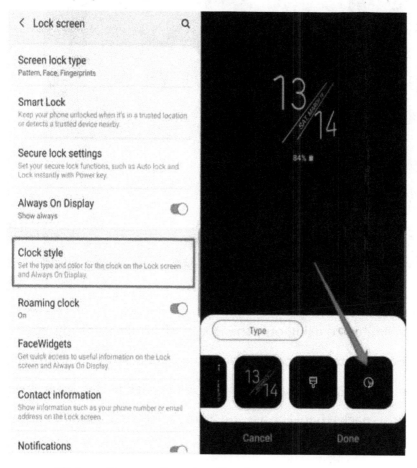

- Click on it once, then tap **Apply.**

- Now go to the **Color** tab, select your preferred color, and click the **Done** button.

- Your new AOD screen is ready.

Stylize the Icons

You are not limited to using only the icon packs from Samsung as you can download several icon packs from Google play store, But you will need to use a third-party launcher like Nova Primes to use these icon packs. The icon packs that I like are the Pixel Pie icon pack and the Voxel icon pack. Do check them out.

But if you prefer the ones from One UI, you can download the icon packs on the Samsung store. To view more packs,

- Long-press on any empty field on the home screen.

- Click on **Themes.**

- Select **Icons.**

- Then click on **Top.**

- Click on your preferred one, download, and click the **Apply** button.

Add a Music Controller to Lock Screen

For music lovers like me, another feature you should have on your lock screen is the music controller. You do not need any third-party app to enjoy this feature. With the music controller enabled, whenever you launch music streaming apps, you will see the controls displayed on the lock screen, and you can also access the app without waking or unlocking your phone.

To enable this feature,

- Go to the settings app.

- Click on **Lock Screen.**

- Select **Face Widgets.**

- Then toggle on the **Music** switch.

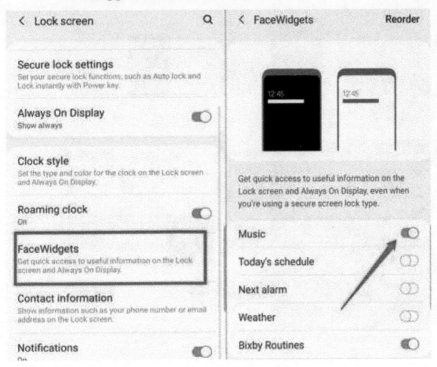

Display Emergency Contact on the Lock Screen

It is only wise to display an emergency contact number on the screen of

your device. To do this,

- Go to settings.

- Click on **Lock Screen.**

- Click on **Contact Information,** set your preferred emergency

  contact.

- The contact details will now show on your lock screen. However, if it doesn't, restart your phone. Double-click on the lock screen to display your wallpaper and the contact.

Lock Home Screen Layout

At times, we move the home screen layout in error. Now you can prevent the home icons from being moved by enabling the Lock Home Screen layout. To do this

- Go to settings.
- Click on **Display**
- Select **Home Screen.**
- Now toggle on the switch for **Lock Home Screen Layout.**
- With this setting in place, you will be unable to move icons within the home screen.

Enable Landscape Mode for Home Screens

While most apps on your Note 20 can switch between the landscape and portrait modes, the home screen remains in portrait mode by default, regardless of how you hold the phone. The steps below will guide you on how to enable landscape mode for your home screen.

- Go to the home screen and long-press on any blank part of the screen.
- Click on **Home Screen Settings.**
- Navigate to **Portrait Mode Only** and move the switch to the left to disable the option.
- Now your home screen can also rotate like other apps.

Quick Settings Panel

The Quick Settings Panel on your device contains shortcuts for device functionality and settings, but you will need to re-arrange the shortcuts for faster access as well as increase the grid size of the shortcuts.

- Swipe down from the top of your phone's display until the Quick Settings Panel covers your screen

- Click on the three-dot ⋮ menu at the top right side of your screen

- Then click on **Button Grid**

- You will see some options displayed at the bottom of the screen. Choose the grid that suits your preference. The 5x3 option can accommodate almost all settings on one pane.

- Now rearrange the icons to your preference using the **Button Order** option from the same view.

- The first six shortcuts you choose will be visible whenever you access the notification pane

- Tap **Done** once satisfied.

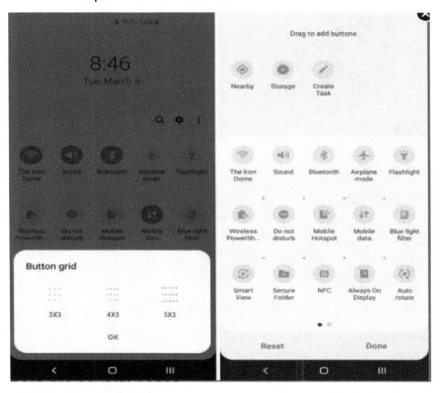

Accommodate More App Icons on the Home screen Grid
You can adjust the home screen app grid to accommodate more app icons on the screen of your device.

- Return to the home screen and long-press on any blank area there.
- Then click on **Home Screen Settings** at the bottom of your screen

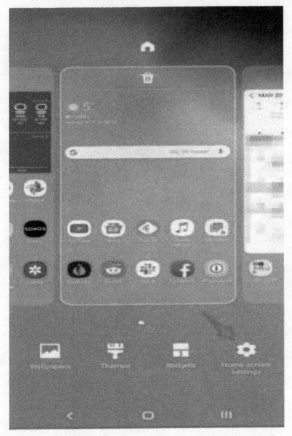

- Click on **Home Screen Grid** and modify the grid size to suit your preference.
- To adjust the app screen grid, follow the steps above to access the **Home Screen Settings,** then click on '**App Screen Grid**' and adjust to your preference.

Activate Navigation Gestures

If you are yet to join the gestures party, follow the steps below

- Open the Settings app.

- Click on **Display.**

- Select **Navigation Bar.**

- Then click on **Full-Screen Gestures** to activate

- You can also click on **button buttons** to change the button order.

- After this is enabled, you can always swipe up from the left side of your screen to pull up the Overview selection.

- Swipe up from the bottom right side of your screen to go back.

- To go to the home screen, swipe up from the middle of the screen.

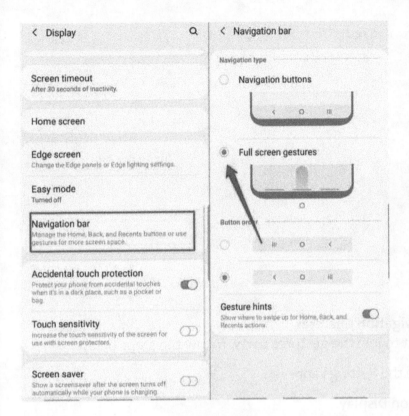

Explore the Overview Selection Mode

The operating system of the Note 20 makes it easy to access some controls like Split Screen, App Info, or Pop up view. Now, rather than diving into settings, you can find the options in the Overview Selection section, also known as Recent Menu. To access these controls,

- Launch the Recent menu
- Click on the desired app icon

Using Samsung Finder

If you are switching from other phone brands to Samsung, you will notice that some of the options and features are hidden in obscure places. Even users who are familiar with the Samsung phones may find some of the menus confusing. Luckily, you can use the Finder app to search for anything on your device, including apps.

- Drag down the notification bar.
- Click on the magnifying glass icon.
- Then type your search term or keyword into the search bar. The option will display modified results as you type.

- You can edit what apps you want to exclude from the search results by clicking on the three vertical dots ⋮ at the right top side of your screen. Then tap **Manage Apps** and customize as you like.

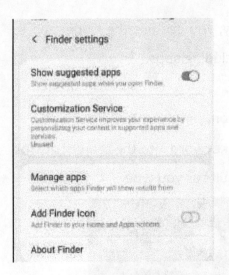

Add Finder to Home Screen

Most Samsung users will agree that the Finder is one of the best features of this operating system. This feature allows you to search for calendar events, settings, and apps. The good news is that you can customize the Finder settings as you like. But one of its most useful settings is the shortcut settings. To add the Finder Shortcut to your home screen,

- Open the app drawer.

- Click on the 3-dot menu in the search button.

- Then click on **Finder Settings.**

- Click on **Add Finder**

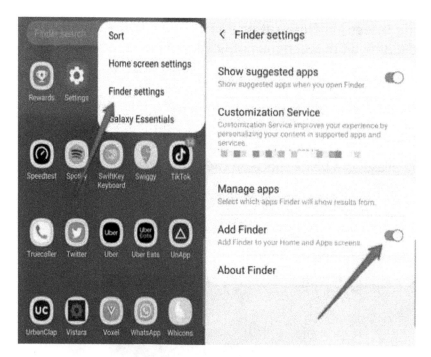

- On the next screen, drag the 1 x 1 icon to the home screen (see screenshot) or tap **Add** to complete.

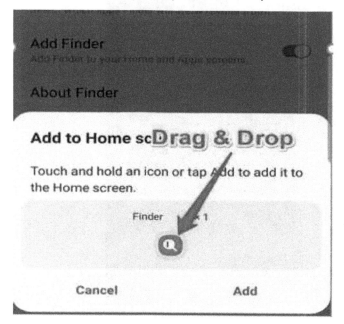

Tweak Home Screen For Notification Panel

Do you find it difficult to reach the notification panel? It will be so much easier if a downward swipe on your home screen can display all the notifications, and yes, there is a way to enable this. To enable this setting,

- Long-press on a blank space on the home screen.

- Then click on **Home Screen Settings.**

- On the next page, navigate to **Quick-Open Notification Panel** and toggle on the switch .

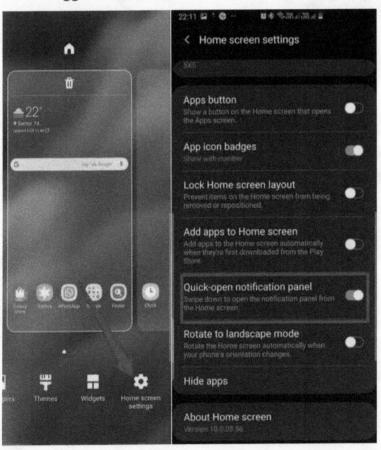

Chapter 7: App Settings

Uninstall an App

To uninstall an app and remove it from your phone,

- Press down on the app that you want to delete. Then click on **Uninstall** from the pop-up menu.

Disable an App

You will be unable to delete system apps but you can disable them with the steps below:

- Press down on the app that you want to disable. Then click on **Disable** from the pop-up menu.

- Click on **Disable** again to finish.

Change Default Apps

By default, the Galaxy note has default apps for performing certain transactions like browsing the web. But you can modify this list of default apps to suit your preference. For instance you can use Chrome browser instead of the Samsung Internet browser.

- Open the **Settings** app and tap **Apps.**

- Tap ⋮ by the top right side of your screen, then select **Default Apps.**

- Click on an App in the **Default App** screen, then select the default app for that category.

Clear Default Apps

If you do not want to have a default app for launching an application or performing an action on your phone, you can clear the default app settings. Each time you attempt to perform or open a file, your phone will ask you to choose an app for that purpose.

- Open the **Settings** app and tap **Apps.**
- Tap the app that you wish to clear the default settings, tap **Set as Default,** then click on **Clear Defaults** to complete.

Show App Suggestions in Recent Apps

Another feature of the One UI is the 'Recent Apps Suggestion,' which is different from the apps' suggestion in the app drawer. This particular feature shows you all the apps you used recently. To use this feature, simply pull up the Recents menu, also known as the **Overview section,** and you will see all your frequently used apps at the bottom of your screen. Of course, you need to enable this feature before you can use it.

- Launch the Recents menu.

- Click on the 3-dot ⋮ button at the right top side of your screen

- Click on **Settings.**

- Then enable the option for **Suggested Apps.**

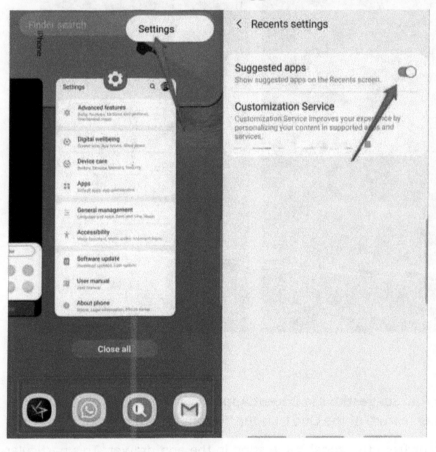

Chapter 8: Manage Google Assistant on Note 20

On the one hand, you have Bixby as Samsung's digital assistant, on the other hand, you have the Google assistant for android phones. You can also install Alexa to give you a third option.

Accessing the Google Assistant

This feature is in sync with your Google account, so it works with anything you previously set-up Google Assistant to do. To access this virtual assistant,

- Long-press on the on-screen home button to launch the Google assistant.

- Now speak to Google to get your search results

Access Google Assistant without the Home Button

For those who set up their device to use gestures instead of the navigation bar,

- Swipe and hold from the bottom middle of the screen, the part where the home button should be.
- You will then see the Google Assistant pop-up

Alternatively, you can enable **OK Google** to activate Voice for the Google Assistant. To do this,

- Launch the Google app.
- Click on the 3-dot ⋮ menu on the top left.
- Click on **Settings.** Select **Voice.**
- Then click on **"Ok Google" Detection.**
- Toggle on the options for **'From Any Screen'** and **'From Google Search App.'**
- Return to the Voice screen and ensure that your Language is set to English (US). And you are done

Make a Call with Google Assistant

- Launch the Google Assistant and say **"Call,"** followed by the receiver's name or the number you wish to call.
- The assistant will then dial the number

Send a Message with Google Assistant

- Launch the Google Assistant and say **"Message,"** followed by the saved contact's name or the number you wish to send the message to as well as the content of the message.

- Then say **Send**

Search with Google Assistant
- Launch the Google Assistant and say your search terms. You will see your results displayed on the screen.

Get Direction with Google Assistant
- Launch the Google Assistant and say **"Directions To,"** followed by the location or address.
- The direction will pop-up on the map.

Open an App with Google Assistant
- Launch the Google Assistant and say **"Open,"** followed by the name of the app

Disable Google Assistant
To remove the Google assistant from the home button shortcut, follow the steps below:
- Go to Settings.
- Click on **Apps.**
- Click on the 3-dot ⋮ menu at the top right of your screen.
- Select **Default Apps.**
- Now click on **Device Assistance App.**
- Then click on **Device Assistance App** again and set the option to **None.**
- So when next you long-press on the home button, nothing will happen

Change Your Digital Assistant to Alexa

You can choose to use Alexa as your digital assistant rather than the Google Assistant. First, install the Alexa app, then follow the steps below to set it up as your default virtual assistant:

- Go to Settings.
- Click on **Apps.**
- Click on the 3-dot ⋮ menu at the top right side of your screen
- Select **Default apps.**
- Now click on **Device Assistance App.**
- Then click on **Device Assistance App** again and choose **Alexa.**

Chapter 9: Bixby

Bixby is Samsung's virtual assistant, different from the Google Assistant, Siri, and Alexa. Samsung designed the virtual assistant to attempt to anticipate what your needs are and send you contextualized reminders. Bixby can send messages, edit photos, compose emails, remind you of important dates, all on command. The virtual assistant also controls some smart home devices like your TVs, smart fridges, and several Samsung devices. We will look at everything you need to know about Bixby

Using Bixby
It is straightforward to pull up Bixby and Bixby Voice. To do this, simply press and hold your power button and the virtual assistant will pop-up.

Changing Bixby Settings
The Note 20 series comes loaded with the three versions of the virtual assistant: Bixby Vision, Bixby Home, and Bixby Voice. Here, we will talk about where to find each setting.

To access Bixby Home,

- Swipe right across your home screen.

To access the settings for your interactive cards,

- Click the 3-dot ⋮ menu in the top right
- Then click on **Cards.**
- Now add the cards (apps) you want to see or remove the ones you do not want to see.

To change the email address linked to your Bixby Home,

- Click the 3-dot ⋮ menu in the top right

- Then click on **Settings.**

- On the next screen, change the email address. You can also change the content providers mapped to your Bixby Home on this screen. (This option allows you to send your location data to specific apps to give helpful and customized data.

Bixby Voice
This part of Bixby houses most of the settings. To access it,

- long-press your power button.

- Now click on the 3-dot ⋮ icon to discover further options like **Quick Commands, Tutorials, and Settings.**

- Click on **Settings** to modify everything from whether Bixby should respond when your phone is locked to your Voice Style.

- Click on **Quick Command** to tie phrases and actions together. For instance, you can customize the virtual assistant to set the alarm and put off all lights when you say, " I am going to bed."

But first, you need to install the software and complete the Bixby's Voice tutorial before you can invoke the voice assistant. You can activate Bixby Voice by saying "Hey Bixby" or pressing down the Bixby button while you talk. You can also customize Bixby Voice like changing the gender of the assistant, shortening lengthy commands to a single phrase or word, etc.

Bixby Marketplace

This feature allows you to customize your Bixby experience further. You can easily add new services, referred to as 'capsules,' as well as check what you can do with the existing capsules. To go to the marketplace,

- Open Bixby.
- Then swipe left to go to the Bixby Marketplace.
- When you get into the marketplace, you can browse through the available categories or search for specific capsules.

Using Bixby Routines
This feature was introduced in Galaxy S10 Plus, wherein the digital assistant studies your behavior and offers ways you can save more time. The suggestions can range from launching apps that meet specific requirements to tweaking system settings.

Also, you can add your customized routines. With this feature, you can program your phone to behave in a defined manner. So, you can set your device to default to silent mode when the clock strikes 9 PM.

To explore this feature,

- Go to Settings.
- Click on **Advanced Features.**
- Then tap on **Bixby Routines.**

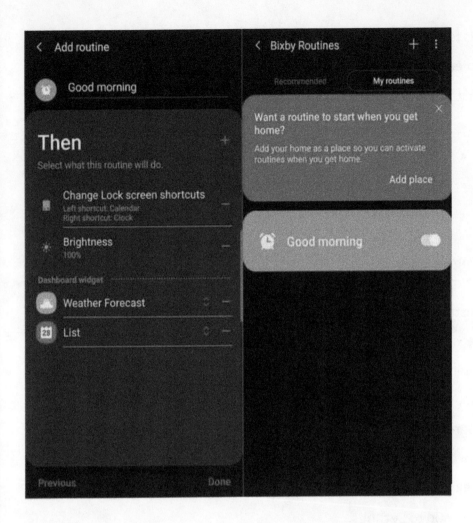

Bixby Vision

Samsung integrated Bixby with your Internet, camera, and gallery apps to present you with a deeper understanding of the things you see.

Camera

Bixby vision is present on the camera viewfinder to help with a better understanding of what you see.

- Open the camera app

- Click on **More**

- Tap **Bixby Vision** ◎

- Then follow the prompts on your screen.

Gallery

Bixby Vision can also be used on images and pictures stored in the gallery app

- Open the gallery app

- Click on a picture to view it

- Click on **Bixby Vision** ◎

- Then follow the prompts on your screen

Internet

You can use Bixby Vision to find out more about an image in the internet app.

- Go to the internet.

- Click and hold an image until a pop-up shows on your screen.

- Click on **Bixby Vision** ◎ .

- Then follow the prompts on your screen.

Remove Bixby From Home Screen

If you are among the group that finds the virtual assistant intrusive, the first step you should take would be to remove the Bixby Home from your home screen.

To do this,

- Long press on the home screen

- Then swipe to the right until you get to a preview of Bixby Home
- Toggle off the switch beside **Bixby Home.**

Remap Bixby Button

You can configure the Bixby button on your device to launch other apps

outside Bixby.

- Double-press the Side button to launch Bixby.

- Click on the 3-dot ⋮ menu icon
- Tap **Settings**
- Then click on **Bixby Key.**

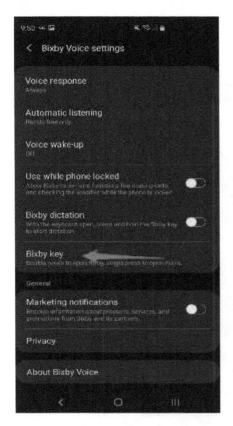

Now, you can set the Bixby key to perform two functions. You can set up the double press or single press option to activate Samsung's personal assistant while you use the remaining settings to open any other app of your choice.

For instance, if you set Bixby to open whenever you single-press the Side key, you can set the double-press option to open Instagram, Twitter, or any other app of your choice.

If you do not want to use the key to launch any app, you can use it to trigger a Bixby Quick Command. Quick Command houses various device actions like reading your calendar, enabling always-on-display, and disabling DND. While these options are prebuilt into Bixby, you can go ahead to create your own commands.

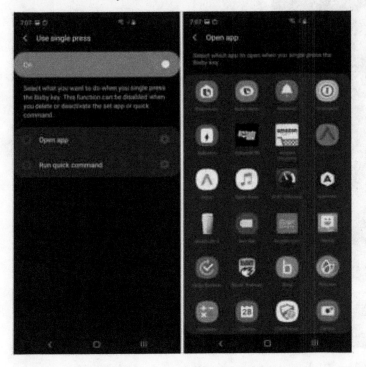

Turn off Bixby Voice wake-up and listening
If you do not want Bixby to wake up your device or you want to prevent Bixby from listening to you, you can turn off the options, only if you previously set up Bixby.

- Open Bixby.
- Click on the menu button at the top right side of your screen
- Select **Settings.**
- On this screen, you will find the option for **Voice Wake-up** and **Automatic Listening.** Turn off both options to disable them.

Chapter 10: The Edge Screen

Using the Edge Panel

The Edge panel contains selected apps that you can access by swiping from the right-hand edge of your screen. Although the edge panel has some apps by default, you can modify the settings to include your favorite apps, and you can also change how this feature works.

- Go to the settings app.
- Click on **Display.**
- Tap **Edge Screen.**
- Then click on **Edge Panels.**
- On the next screen, you can choose to disable the feature completely, use clipboard or weather information only or select the apps or contacts that you want to show up in this view

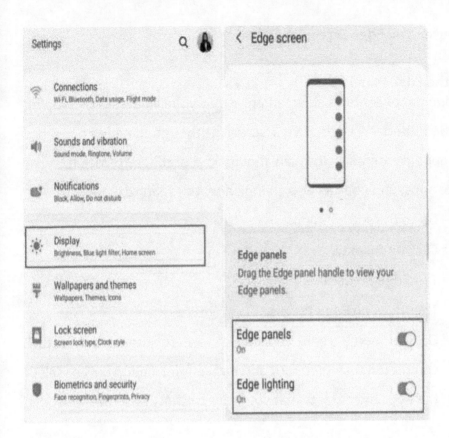

Brighten Up Your Notifications with Edge Lighting

Another exciting way to use your device's screen edges is to have them light up whenever a notification arrives. The light will replace the usual pop-up alerts and works well even when your phone is face down. To enable this feature,

- Go to the settings app
- Click on **Display.**
- Tap **Edge Screen.**
- Then click on **Edge Lighting.**

- In this screen, you can disable or enable the feature, selectively activate edge lights for specific apps, choose your preferred lighting light, and lots more.

Tweak Edge Handles

One way you can handle your phone with one hand is to organize the Edge screen's handles to suit your convenience. This handle is usually located at the right edge of the Samsung screen by default, but you can always customize to suit your convenience.

- Pull out the Edge screen.
- Click on the settings icon at the left lower side of your screen.
- Then click on the 3-dot ⋮ menu at the top of the screen.
- Now select **Edge Panel Handle.**

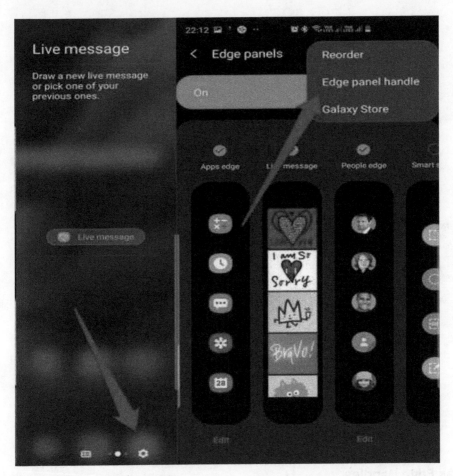

- On the next screen, you can change the position, transparency, size, and position of the handle.

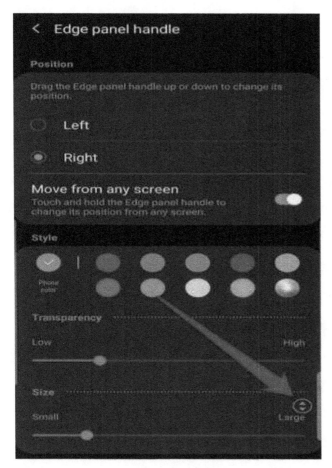

You may also reorder the panels to suit your convenience. To achieve this,

- Return to the previous page

- Click on the 3-dot ⋮ icon again

- Then select **Reorder.**

Chapter 11: Camera/ Video Tips

The camera of the Note 20 comes loaded with hidden settings and features which we will explore in this chapter.

Shoot 8k Video on Galaxy Note 20

Thanks to the Snapdragon 865 chipset and the all-new camera sensors, you can shoot 8K videos on your phone. Now you can shoot videos that have 4 times the amount of pixels of the 4K. One interesting note about 8K video recording is that you can pull 33MP stills directly from the video. There is no limit to how much you can shoot, so long as you have enough storage on your phone.

Some important things to Note about shooting in 8K: You can only shoot in a 16:9 format, and the frame rate is stuck at 24 frames per second while shooting at 4K gives you 60 frames per second. Notwithstanding, the 8K video is still exciting, and you should try it on your new Note 20. Let us begin with how to shoot 8k video on your device:

- Open the camera app.
- Switch to **Video** mode.

- Click on the **Video Ratio button,** then click on **9:16 8K** to activate 8K video recording
- You can now click the **Record** button on the viewfinder to begin shooting your 8K video

Edit 8K Videos

The default video editor of the Note 20 allows you to easily edit 8K footage shot on your phone, straight from the camera interface.

- After shooting the video, click on the video thumbnail on the left side of the camera interface.

- Click on the **Edit button.**

- Click on **Allow** to grant the Video editor access to your device's storage

- Now proceed to make the necessary editing from the editor's interface. You can choose to include emoji, effects and filters, trim video length, and add text. Note that when you add emoji effects or text to your video, it will convert the video to 4K.

Shoot 108MP Photo

The Note 20 Ultra has the 108MP Ultra-wide rear camera lens while the Note 20 has the 64MP rear camera lens. You can shoot your photos using the 108 or 64MP lens.

- Open the Camera app and stay on the Photo mode.
- Tap the ratio icon at the top of your screen.
- Tap either **3:4 (108 MP High Resolution) or 3:4 (64 MP)**.

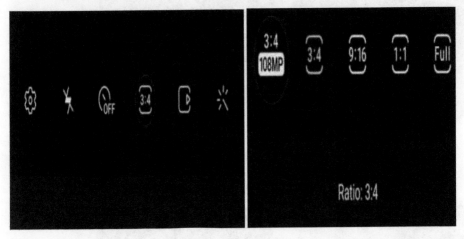

- Tap the Shutter button at the bottom of your screen to capture your photo.

Capture Pro Image/ Video

Pro Mode on your camera app gives you advanced features like the ISO, shutter speed, etc. These features allow you to tweak and customize your photo to give you different feel.

- Open the Camera app and swipe right till you get to the end of your screen.

- Tap **More,** then tap 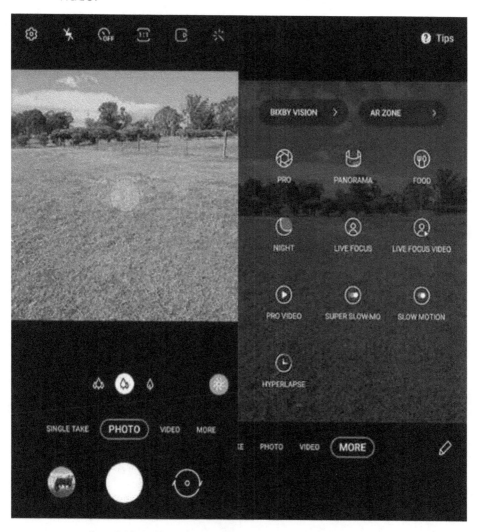**Pro** for photos and **Pro Video** for video.

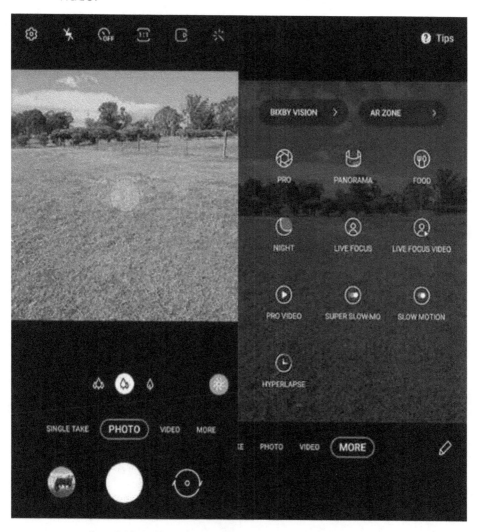

- Tap the different camera settings and customize as desired.

  - **ISO** is used to adjust the light sensitivity of your camera.

- **Aperture & Shutter Speed** is used to control your shutter speed.

- **Standard** is used to modify the shadows, color temperature, saturation and highlights of your image.

- **Manual Focus** to manually change the focus mode.

- **White Balance** is used to modify the white balance of your camera.

- **Exposure** is used to control the amount of light that the camera sensor has.

- Make all necessary changes, then tap the shutter button to capture your photo.

Shoot with Ultra-wide Camera

The Ultra-wide camera lens captures more scene than the wide-angle camera. Follow the steps below to use this camera lens:

- Open the Camera app and stay on the Photo mode.

- You will find three icons close to the bottom of your screen. Tap to switch to the ultra-wide camera. Tap for wide-angle lens and ⬩ for the telephoto camera lens.

Shoot Live Focus Photo

Use the Live Focus camera mode if you want to capture an image or photo where the subject stands out in a blurry background. After you shoot the video or photo, you can also modify the blur level.

- Open the Camera app and swipe to **Live Focus.**

- Ensure that your subject fits into the camera frame, then tap the

   icon at the bottom left side of your viewfinder.

- Tap the individual buttons to get your desired feel.

- Drag the Blur slider to the left or right to adjust the blur level.

- Tap the Shutter button to capture your image.

Shoot Live Focus Videos

- Open the Camera app and swipe right till you get to the end of your screen.

- Tap **More,** then tap **Live Focus Video.**

- Select the Live Focus video effect that you like.

- Drag the Blur slider to the left or right to adjust the blur level.

- Tap the record button to begin your video.

Shoot Hyperlapse Videos

Use Hyperlapse Video mode to create your personal time-lapse video. Tap on Night Hyperlapse to capture your video in an environment without proper lighting or when you shoot at night.

- Open the Camera app and swipe right till you get to the end of your screen.

- Tap **More,** then tap 🕐 **Hyperlapse.**

- Use the ⒸA icon at the top right of your phone screen to customize your video speed.
- This will launch another option at the top of your phone screen.

  - ⒸA icon best used to read high-speed videos.

  - Ⓒ4x use to record active people.

  - Ⓒ8x for traffic or slow-moving videos.

  - Ⓒ16x best used to record clouds in the sky.

  - Ⓒ32x best used to capture crowd of people.

  - Ⓒ64x for sunrise and sunsets.

- Select your desired options, then use the back arrow to go to the previous screen.

- If shooting at night, click on the 🌙 icon for Night Hyperlapse mode.

- Click the record button to start recording your video.

Smart Selfie Angle
This camera mode is used when taking a selfie that involves more people. The feature displays two zoom buttons that ensure that more people are covered in the selfie.

- Open the Camera app and check that you are on the Photo mode.

- Tap the gear icon ⚙ at the top left of your phone screen.

- Move the switch beside **Smart Selfie Angle** to the right to enable.

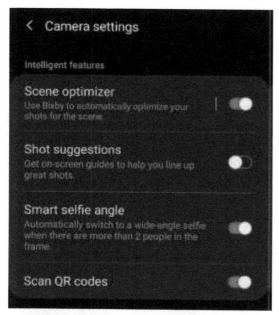

Single Take

One single capture can give you up to 14 different photo and video formats. The Single Take mode captures in the form of a video recording. At the end of the recording, you will have cropped images, filtered images, stills, slow-mo videos and other camera formats just from the single clip.

- Open the Camera app, then swipe to the left to go to **Single Take.**
- Tap the shutter button to start.
- At the end of the recording, you will find the preview thumbnail at the bottom left of your viewfinder. Click on the thumbnail to view all the formats of the recording. Pull the icon upward to display all the formats of your recording.

114

- If you find any video or photo that you wish to save, tap **Select,** then choose the images/ videos and tap the down-arrow icon to store them.

Burst Shots

Burst shot allows you to capture up to 100 different shots when shooting a sped-up moment or a fast-moving object.

- In the camera app, press the shutter button, and pull it down to the right side of your screen. Continue to hold the shutter button until you are satisfied with your shot count.

Capture GIFs Images

By default, pressing the shutter button and pulling it down to the right bottom side of your phone screen will take burst shots. However, you can also use this option to take GIFs instead. This is how to make the switch.

- Open the Camera app and while in Photo mode, tap the gear 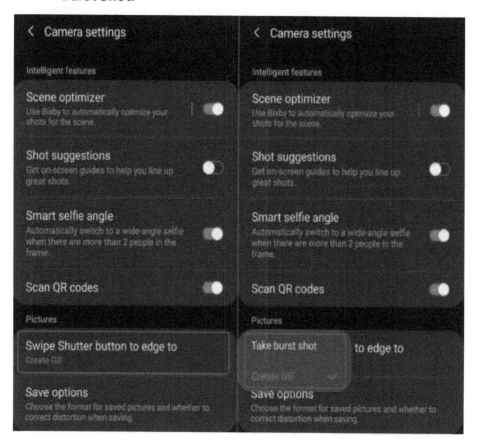 icon.

- Tap **Swipe Shutter Button to Edge to** and choose **Create GIF** or **Burst Shot.**

Quickly Record Video

To quickly record video from any camera mode outside the Video mode,

- Press down on the shutter button. Continue to hold the button until you are done with the recording.

High-Efficiency Video

This feature is enabled to ensure that your videos do not take plenty of spaces. While the option is automatically enabled for 8K videos, you will need to enable it manually when shooting 4K video.

- Open the Camera app, then swipe right to **Video.**

- Tap the gear icon by the top left of your phone screen.

- Tap **Advanced Recording Options,** then move the switch beside **High-Efficiency Video** to the right to enable it.

Extend the Timer

The Galaxy Note 20 allows you to record super slow-mo videos for either 0.8 seconds or 0.4 seconds. Recording on a 0.4 seconds option gives the best results while that of 0.8 seconds maintains standard quality. 0.8 seconds of video captured at 480 fps will yield 24 seconds of playback while 0.4 seconds of video at 960 fps will produce 12 seconds of playback time.

To shoot your super slow-mo videos using either of the options,

- Open the Camera app and swipe right till you get to the end of your screen.

- Tap **More,** then tap **Super Slow-mo.**

- Click on the timer icon at the top of your screen and choose either 0.8 or 0.4.

- Tap 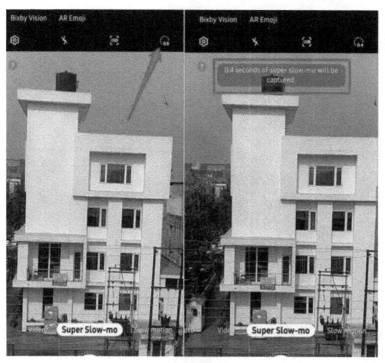 to activate **Motion Detection.**

- Press the shutter button to capture your photo.

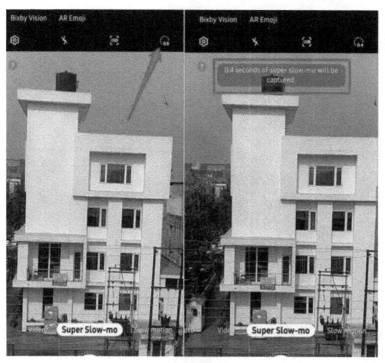

Customize Slow Motion Videos

Just like the S20, the Note 20 has two time-frames for capturing slow-motion videos: 0.8 and 0.4 seconds. Simply click on the timer at the right upper side of your screen and select your preferred option. You also need to ensure that the Auto Detect mode is active. As the name implies, this feature ensures that recording begins when the camera detects any action/ movement.

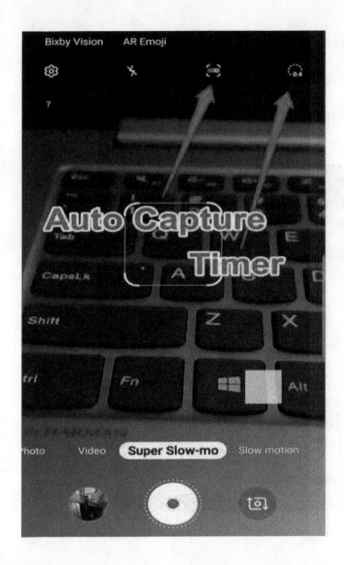

Adjust the Motion Detection Box

With Motion Detection enabled, the camera will wait for a movement or action within the detection box before it starts recording. But there may be instances where the action happens so fast that the camera is unable to detect on time, thereby missing some critical part in the recording. To handle situations like this, simply increase the size of the focus by dragging the edges of the box to expand the coverage.

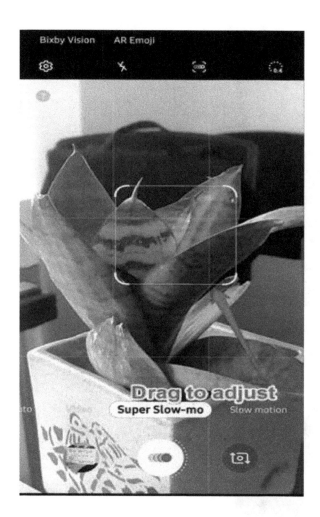

Enable Scene Optimizer

The scene optimizer of the Note 20 series can differentiate between pets and buildings, optimize images accordingly, among many other things. To enable this feature,

- Launch the camera app.

- Go to the settings by clicking on the cog-shaped icon 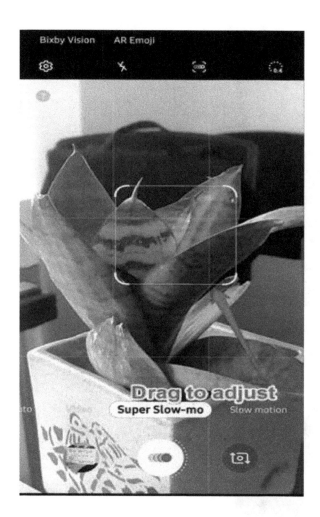.

- Then toggle on the switch for **Scene optimizer**

- With this feature enabled, a powder blue icon will appear each time you launch the camera app.

- To disable the feature, just click on the blue icon.

That's not all. Apart from recognizing scenes, the scene optimizer also performs other functions like Starburst and Document scan. Starburst converts burst of light on low-light photos to artistic effects while the Document scan, like the name implies, scans documents. To activate,

- Click on **Scene optimizer**

- Then toggle the switch for both the **Starburst** and **Document scan.**

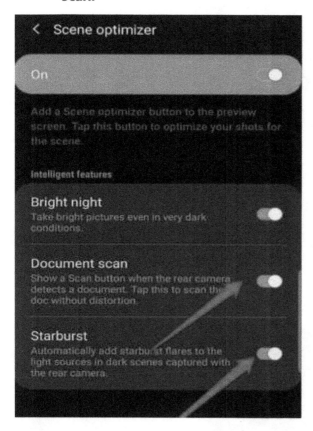

Activate Shot Suggestion

This is another exciting feature of the Note 20 camera. The camera uses the AI prowess of the device to detect scenarios and offer you suggestions on ways to get better shots.

Once enabled, you will see two guiding orbs on your screen (one for improving composition and the other for straightening). All you now have to do is align the focus with the orbs and take your shot.

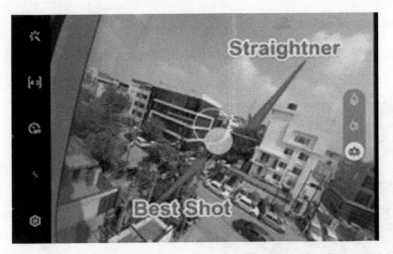

The camera app may take a few seconds to analyze the shot. To enable the shot suggestion feature,

- Launch the camera app.

- Go to the settings by clicking on the cog-shaped icon .

- Then toggle on the switch for **Shot suggestions**

Explore the Food Mode

This mode is an interesting one for foodies as it will not only capture the very minute details of the subject but will also give the image a rich tone. You can also use this mode to capture other colorful items to bring out their full glory. You have two ways to achieve this; either you keep the whole image in focus, or you highlight a specific area. I always prefer the first option.

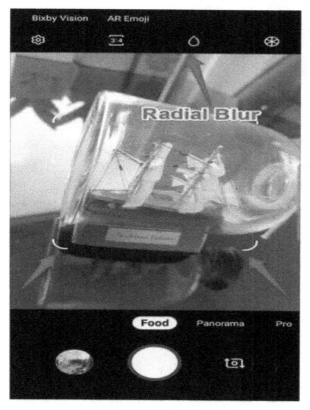

Another exciting feature is the Pallete, which you can use to adjust the color and temperature of your image. Simply drag the slider until you get the best of the image.

Both the Pallete and the Radial blur are available on the tools ribbon at the top of your screen.

Automatically Correct Wide-Angle Shots
Owing to the ultra-wide mode of the Note 20, you can capture some fantastic wide-angle sots. The device also has a dedicated wide-angle shot correction feature that eliminates lens distortion from the edges of your images.

Distorted window frame

The distortion is removed automatically as soon as the picture is saved.

To activate this option,

- Launch the camera app.

- Go to settings by clicking on the cog-shaped icon

- Click on **Save Options.**

- Enable the option for **Ultra-Wide Shape Correction.**

- On this same screen, enable the **RAW copies** and **HEIF pictures** option.

- The RAW copies will give you a picture (when taken in Pro mode) in RAW image and JPEG formats while the latter helps to save space.

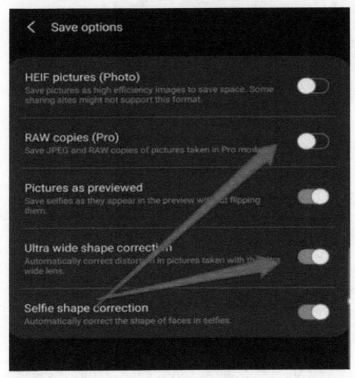

RAW photos record more information than the typical standard JPEG images, thereby making them easy to edit.

Advanced Recording Options

The HDR10+, a high dynamic range format, was first introduced in the Samsung S10. This feature optimizes the contrast and color of videos to make them look more life-like. To enable this feature,

- Launch the camera app and swipe to Video mode.

- Click on settings ⚙.

- Then click on **Advanced Recording Options.**

- Enable the option for **HDR10+ Video**

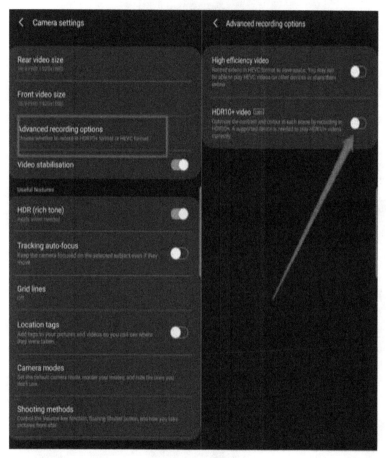

Create Custom Filter
Follow the steps below to create filters using images on your phone.

- In the Photo mode of the camera app, tap the filter ▦ icon at the top of your phone screen.

- Tap **My Filter** and tap **+** at the bottom of your viewfinder.

- On the next screen, select the image that has the filter you wish to use. Click on **Next.**

- Rename the filter and tap **Rename.** Tap **Save Filter** to record your changes.

Add Filter to a Photo

Let me show you how to use filter when shooting your photo:

- Tap the Filter icon ▨ at the top of your screen.

- The next screen will display your recently used filter. Go to **My Filter** for all your filters.

- Select the filter that you want to use. Switch to **Original** to see what the photo will be like without the filter.

- Use the intensity slider to modify the filter.

- Tap the shutter button to take your photo.

Switch on Video Stabilization

The standard telephoto lens and wide camera are optically stabilized lenses, and so, we expect videos should be steady. But, you can take it a step further by activating video stabilization to give you smoother footages. This feature will ensure that your videos are free from wobbles and shakes. To activate,

- Launch the camera app and swipe to Video mode.

- Click on settings ⚙.

- Then enable the option for **Video Stabilization**

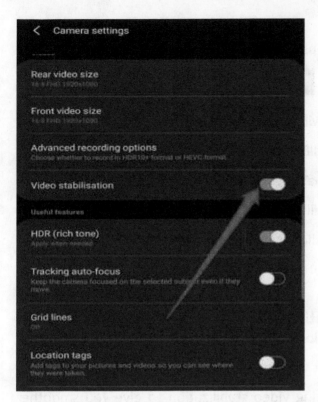

Another great stabilization feature is the **"Super Steady stabilization mode."** Represented by a hand icon in the video mode, the feature helps to capture smooth footages. However, videos under this feature are recorded in 1080p resolution.

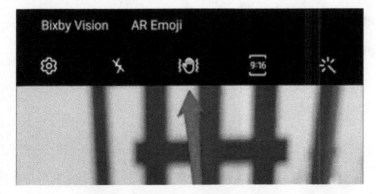

Rearrange Camera Modes

You can arrange your camera mode to have your favorites modes beside each other, like having the Photo mode next to the food mode. To do this,

- Open the camera app.

- Swipe right until you get to the **More** subsection

- Click on the **Edit icon** at the right lower side of your screen

- Pull the desired shooting mode from the sub-menu onto the ribbon.

- The shooting mode should now appear in the camera mode at the bottom of your screen

- Click on **Save** once you are done dragging all the desired camera modes to the camera tray

Here's another way to rearrange the camera mode.

- Launch the camera app
- Click on settings
- Click on **Camera modes**
- Click on **Edit modes**
- Rearrange the modes by dragging each one to the desired position
- Untick the modes you do not use to deactivate them and declutter your camera interface.

Open Last Used Camera Mode

Also, if you want the camera app to open to the last mode you used when next you launch the camera, follow the steps below:

- Launch the camera app.

- Click on Settings ⚙

- Click on **Camera Modes.**

- Then enable the option for **Keep Using Last Mode.**

Use Your Device to Scan Documents

The Samsung Note 20 camera can automatically reduce distortion for any documents scanned on the device, be it bank statements, receipts, letters, etc.

- Open the camera app

- Click on the cog icon to access the app settings

- Select **Scene optimizer** and switch on the option

- Also, confirm that the **Document Scan** is enabled

- Then scan a document using the rear camera of the device to see the optimizations applied.

Take Photos with Palm

You can also take photos on your device without clicking the shutter button. Once you show your palm to the camera, it will automatically take photos. This is especially useful for times you are unable to reach the shutter button but can show your palm to the camera. To enable this feature,

- Go to the camera app.

- Click on the camera settings 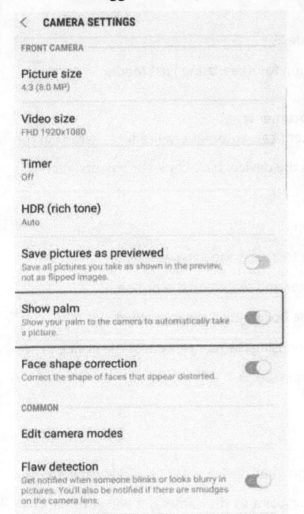.

- Tap **Shooting Methods.**

- Now toggle on the option for **Show Palm**

< CAMERA SETTINGS

FRONT CAMERA

Picture size
4:3 (8.0 MP)

Video size
FHD 1920x1080

Timer
Off

HDR (rich tone)
Auto

Save pictures as previewed
Save all pictures you take as shown in the preview,
not as flipped images.

Show palm
Show your palm to the camera to automatically take
a picture.

Face shape correction
Correct the shape of faces that appear distorted.

COMMON

Edit camera modes

Flaw detection
Get notified when someone blinks or looks blurry in
pictures. You'll also be notified if there are smudges
on the camera lens.

Edit Live Focus Photos

Follow the steps below to edit your live focus images:

- Go to your gallery and open the image.

- Click on the **Change Background Effect** bubble.

- Select the new mode.

- Then click on **Apply**

This also applies to the front camera; the only exception is the frame. The frames of the front camera are a bit wide, mainly due to the use of the main camera for taking portrait shots rather than the telephoto lens.

Edit Super Slow-Mo Video

After shooting your super slow-mo videos, you can edit it with the steps below:

- Launch the video in the gallery app.

- Click on the **Play Super slow-mo video** icon towards the bottom of the screen to launch the video in edit mode.

- Now customize as you desire.

- To change the audio track, click on the little music icon and choose **Theme Music**

- Save your changes once done.

Remove Flickering from Your Videos

To best enjoy slow-motion videos, you need light. The more light you have, the better the quality of your videos. The best time to shoot super slow-motion videos is in the mornings and middays. The video will not only be noise-less but will also eliminate unwanted shadows. But if you notice that your video has slight flickering, you can use a built-in option to remove the flickering.

- Open the video in your phone gallery
- Click on the Play slow-motion video bubble
- Click on the three-dot ⋮ menu at the top right side of your screen.
- Then toggle the switch for **Remove flickering**

Add a Trippy Audio Track

Your Samsung Note 20 allows you to add a trippy song to a video to lift the mood of the video, and this feature comes with several audio tracks. To add a song

- Open the desired video in your Gallery.
- Click on the edit icon .
- Click on the Music bubble above the seek bar.
- If accessing this module for the first time, tap **OK** on the confirmation box.
- Then choose from the available songs

- All the songs in this module are arranged according to categories, making it easy for you to select and download desired songs. Ensure you have good internet coverage as you need to download most tracks before you can successfully use them.

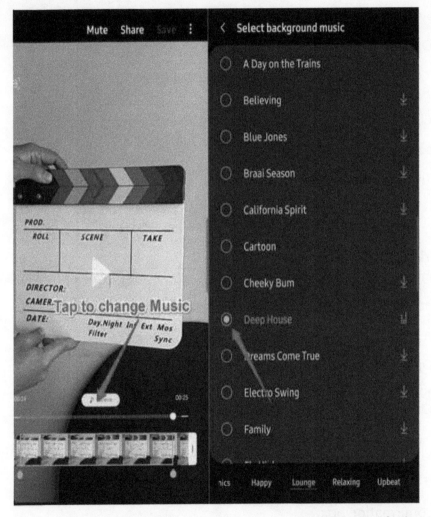

- After downloading, make the other modifications/ adjustments
- Then save it

Loop and Reverse

Your Samsung Note 20 not only allows you to save a super slow-mo video in reverse order, you can also get the same video in a **Forward & Reverse** format.

- Click on the video to launch it.

- Then hit the three-dot ⋮ icon

- Click on **Details.**

- Three clips will display at the bottom of your screen.

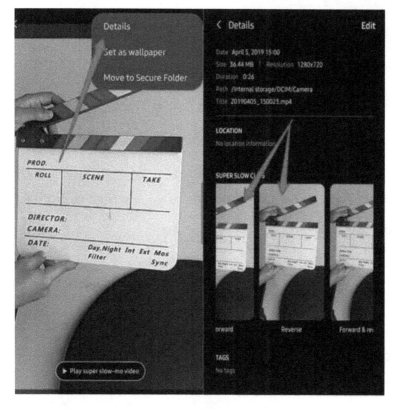

- Click on the one you like and Save as **MP4** or GIF.

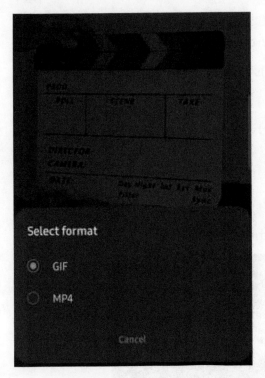

Select format

◉ GIF

○ MP4

Cancel

- You can now perform regular modifications like trimming or adding songs

Tip: click on the camera icon on the right side of your screen to capture a still frame from a video

Hide Albums in Gallery

Another cool feature of the Note 20 series is being able to hide your albums and photos in the Gallery, especially if you have private videos and pictures you do not want others to view. To use this feature,

- Open the gallery app.

- Click on the 3-dot ⋮ menu at the top right corner of your screen.

- Click on **Hide or Unhide**

- Now choose the albums you want to hide.

- Once done, you will no longer see the selected albums in the gallery until you disable this feature.

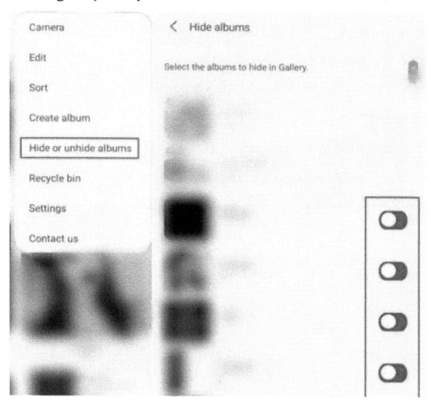

Use Video Wallpaper
To use a video as your lock screen wallpaper, do this:

- Click on the video in the gallery app, then tap the ⋮ menu by the top right side of your phone screen.

- Tap **Set as Wallpaper** to complete setup.

Chapter 13: Audio Experience

Play with Sound Settings (Separate App Sounds)

The Galaxy Note 20 series has another exciting feature known as the Separate App Sounds. This feature allows you to have two different audio outputs from two different apps on your device. For example, you can choose to play your favorite podcast on your wireless speaker instead of the phone's speaker. And it is very easy to set up too.

- Go to settings.
- Click on **Sound and Vibration.**
- Now click on **Separate App Sounds.**
- Then choose the app and the sound output you want.That's all!

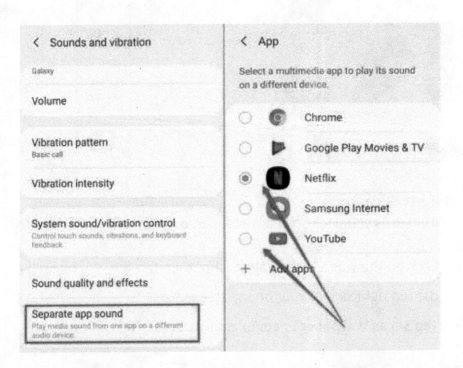

Customize Sound Based on Age

The Note 20 comes with built-in capabilities to tweak the high and low tones to suit your listening preferences. Enabling this feature will help you hear well-detailed and more defined sounds that may otherwise be missing. This feature is known as Adaptive Sound. To enable this feature,

- Go to settings.

- Click on **Sounds and Vibrations.**

- Select **Sound Quality and Effects.**

- Then click on **Adapt Sound.**

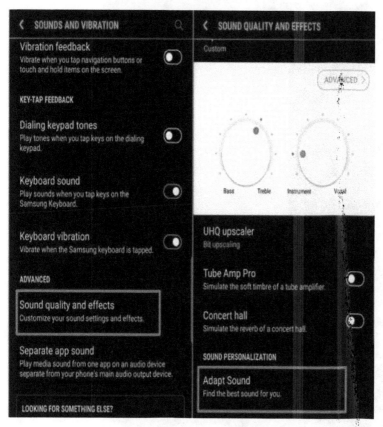

- Create a custom sound profile or choose a readymade profile for your age.

- To create a custom sound profile, click on the **Add Personalized sound** button at the end of your screen.

- Plug-in your earphones and your device will walk you through the process.

- On your screen, you will see the real-time changes in the equalizer. Save the settings once done

- Tap the cog icon if you want to hear the difference between the two profiles.

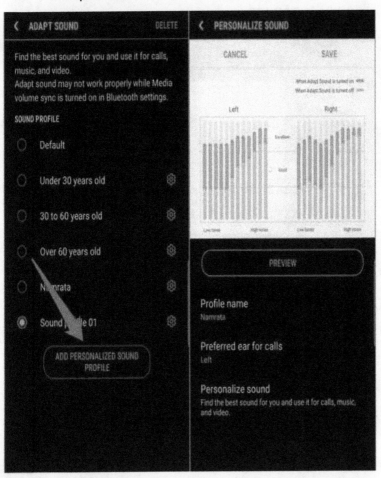

Dolby Atmos

This feature helps to enhance your audio experience by increasing the default volume of your phone by about twenty-five percent while adding special effects at the same time. Another cool thing about this feature is that it has three more profiles for Music, Voices, and Movie.

With the music profile enabled, you will enjoy a clean and rich sound experience while the Voice profile enhances voices in movies or videos, and the Movie profile gives you an immersive experience.

This feature is disabled by default. To enable Dolby Atmos,

- Go to settings
- Click on **Sounds and Vibration**
- Tap **Advanced Sound Settings**
- Click on **Sound Quality and Effects.**
- Enable **Dolby Atmos** by moving the switch to the right.
- You may also enable **Dolby Atmos for Gaming** to have this same audio experience when playing games on your phone.
- To change the sound profile, click on **Dolby Atmos** and select your preference on the next screen

Using UHQ Upscaler

Just like the Dolby Atmos, your phone has dedicated profiles for earphones. When listening to songs on your phone, you can switch between Concert Hall, Tube Amp Pro, and UHQ Upscaler sound setting. UHQ Upscaler comes with DSD and UHQ 32-bit support to ensure that you enjoy higher quality audio.

- Go to settings.

- Click on **Sounds and Vibration.**

- Tap **Advanced Sound Settings.**

- Click on **Sound Quality and Effects.**

- Scroll down on the page and click on **UHQ Upscaler.**

- On the next screen, click on your choice from the two options.

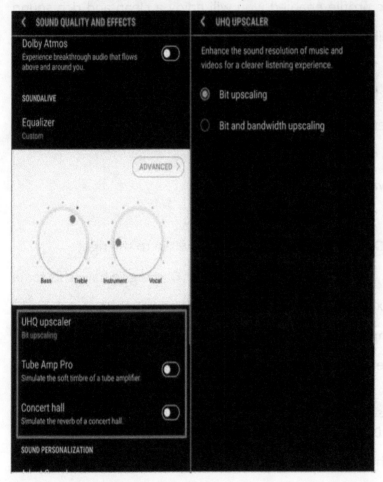

Change Bluetooth Audio Codec

Your Samsung Note 20 supports several Bluetooth audio codecs like

LDAC, aptX, etc. So, if you have a pair of LDAC or aptX HD headphones, you can switch to the profile which your headphones support. But to enjoy this feature, you need to enable the option from the Developer settings on your device.

To unlock the Developer settings

- Go to settings

- Click on **About phone.** Tap **Software Information.**

- Then click on **Build number** 7 times.

- After doing this, use the search bar to search for **Bluetooth Audio Codec**

- A pop-up will display on your screen, change to your choice

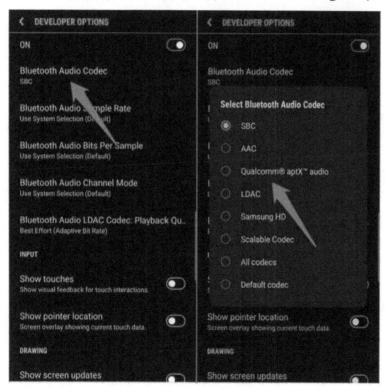

Turn Off Unnecessary Sounds

Your Samsung Note 20 is set by default to make little noises for every time you touch it, and this can be pretty annoying both for the user and everyone else around you. These extra noises and vibration will also drain your battery faster. To turn off this noise

- Go to settings
- Click on **Sounds and Vibration.**
- Tap **System Sounds and Vibrations.**

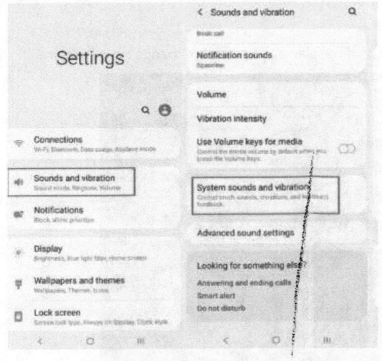

- Then switch off every sound that you do not need.

< System sounds and vibration

System sounds

Touch sound
Play sounds when you touch certain items on the screen.

Screen lock sound
Play sounds when you lock or unlock the screen.

Charging sound
Play sound when your phone starts charging.

Dialing keypad tone
Play tones when you tap the dialing keypad.

Keyboard sound
Play sound when you tap the Samsung Keyboard.

System vibration

Keyboard vibration
Vibrate when you tap the Samsung Keyboard.

Touch vibration
Vibrate when you tap navigation buttons or touch and hold items on the screen.

150

Chapter 14: Explore the Sound Assistant App

The Sound Assistant app is an in-house app designed to tweak the system sounds, and it comes packed with several features. One advantage of this app is the floating audio button that lets you access the sound settings quickly. To enable the sound profiles or set the floating equalizer, all you need to do is click on the button to activate a floating window. Then click on the Settings icon, and you will find all you need. To enable the floating button,

- Launch the Sound Assistant app.
- Toggle on the switch for **Floating** button.
- Click on the card to set how long you want the button to remain on the home screen.
- Then hit any of the volume rocker buttons to see the floating window.

Increase Volume Step
You may have been in a situation where you need to adjust the volume of your device just a little. But when you tap the volume key up, the speakers blast louder than you want. The default Samsung volume steps are 15, which most users are okay with. But for users who do not fancy the Samsung default volume steps, you can try the Volume Steps feature. To activate this feature,

- Go to the Advanced settings of the SoundAssistant app.
- Drag the slider for step volume to your preferred number.

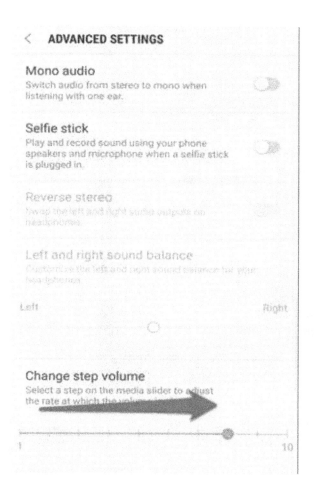

Save and Share EQ Settings

Your device allows you to share your equalizer settings with friends, thanks to the SoundAssistant app. To do this,

- Bring up the floating equalizer window for SoundAssistant app.

- Adjust your settings as desired and save it.

- Then click on the share icon to share with friends.

Manage Volume for Individual Apps

Again, the SoundAssistant app helps you to assign individual volume to several multimedia apps. With this feature, you can increase the volume for YouTube videos to the highest while keeping that of Google Music at 5%.

The first step is to add the apps

- Launch the SoundAssistant app.
- Select individual app volume options.
- Add the apps and modify the volume to your preference.
- When next you launch the modified apps, the volume will revert to the one you set in the SoundAssistant app.

- To decrease or increase the volume for an app, launch the SoundAssitant floating window, click on the Arrow icon and pull the slider for each of the apps.

Personalize Sound Profiles

The key feature of the SoundAssistant app is to personalize sound profiles as it allows you to set individual volume levels for different times in a day. For example, you can set your phone to be on silent mode at 8 a.m once you enter the office and revert to normal mode at 6 p.m. to do this,

- Launch the SoundAssistant app.

- Click on **Scenarios** and edit as you want.

- Click on **Save** once done.

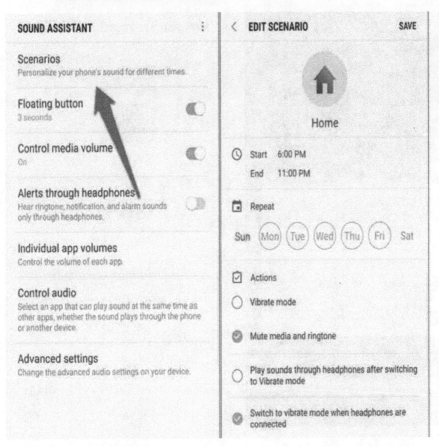

Chapter 15: Samsung Pay

Samsung Pay is a digital wallet and mobile payment service from Samsung that you can use to make purchases in any store that accepts the service. The good news is that Samsung Pay is accepted in most stores in the USA. It is a safe and easy way to make payments without carrying physical cards.

Setup Samsung Pay
- A swipe up from the bottom of your screen will launch the Samsung Pay app.
- Tap **Get Started,** then choose a safe PIN in the next screen. Re-enter the PIN when prompted.
- In the Samsung Pay app, tap **+ Credit/ Debit** to add a debit or credit card.
- Chose the card type then follow the prompts on your screen to confirm the card.

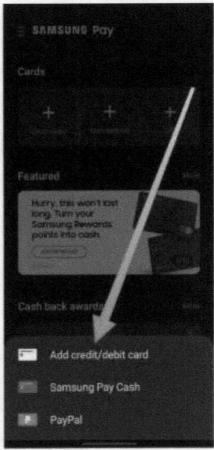

- To add a membership card from accepted stores, tap
  +Membership on the Samsung App home screen, tap the name
  of the store or click on **Add a Card Not Listed Here** if the store
  isn't listed.

- To load or buy a gift card, tap **+Gift,** then click on **Load Gift Cards** or **Buy Gift Cards.** If loading gift card, tap the gift card vendor or search for the vendor, then follow the prompts on your screen to complete. If buying a gift card, tap the vendor for the gift card you want to buy, then follow the prompts to complete.

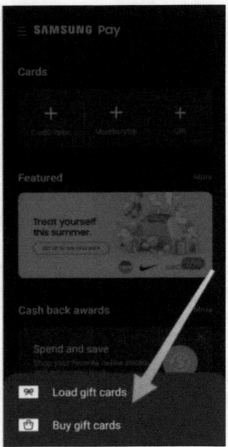

Authorize Purchases with Fingerprint

Apart from the PIN you entered during set up, you can activate the fingerprint option to authorize purchases using the registered fingerprint rather than the PIN.

- Launch Samsung Pay.
- Tap **Menu** by the left top side of your phone screen.
- Tap **Settings,** then move the switch beside **Fingerprint** to the right to enable it.

Pay with Samsung Pay

At the checkout point, here is how to complete or authorize your purchases:

- Tap **Pay** on the Samsung Pay app. Select the card that should be debited, then enter your PIN or place your registered fingerprint on the fingerprint scanner to confirm the payment.

- Tap the back of your Galaxy Note against the merchant terminal to complete your payment.

- If the payment is successful, you will receive a notification that shows the amount and the name of the merchant.

Chapter 16: Device Security

In-Display Ultrasonic Fingerprint Scanner

The Note 20 comes with an in-display ultrasonic fingerprint scanner that is accurate and fast. To unlock your smartphone, simply place your thumb on the lock screen. Note 20 requires every owner to use the ultrasonic fingerprint scanner. The steps below will guide you on how to set up the fingerprint lock:

- Go to **Settings.**
- Click on **Biometrics and Security.**
- Select **Fingerprints.**
- Now click on **Add Fingerprints** and set up your fingerprint.

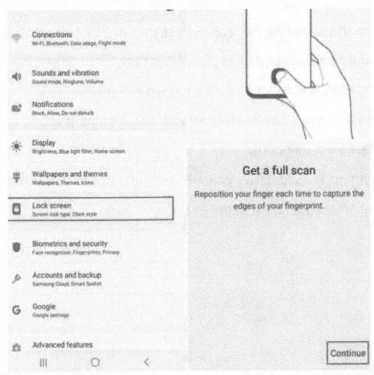

Enable Fingerprint Icon

The in-display fingerprint scanner is one of the coolest features in Note 20. It is not only fast but also accurate. But one problem with this scanner is that it is easy to miss it, mainly when the display is off. In cases like this, your best bet is to activate the Fingerprint scanner icon. Note 20 makes the icon visible when you tap your phone screen, even when the screen is off. To enable this feature,

- Go to Settings.

- Click on **Biometrics and Security.** Select **Fingerprints.**

- Move the switch beside **'Show icon when the screen is off'** to the right to enable it.

- You can disable this option once you can tell its location.

- To unlock your phone, tap once on your device screen, then press your thumb against the screen.

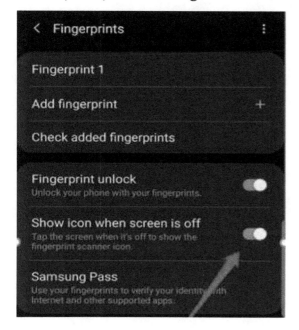

The Alternate Look Feature

It's 2020! Several phone users are familiar with the face recognition feature that unlocks a locked screen in seconds. Yet, there are still some glitches with using this feature when you put on accessories like wearing dark-tinted sunglasses. Samsung's One UI 2.0 has addressed this issue with the new Alternate Look feature. With this feature enabled, your phone will recognize you even with accessories on. To activate this feature,

- Go to settings.
- Click on **Biometric and Security.**
- Click on **Face Recognition.**
- Then click on **Add Alternative Look**

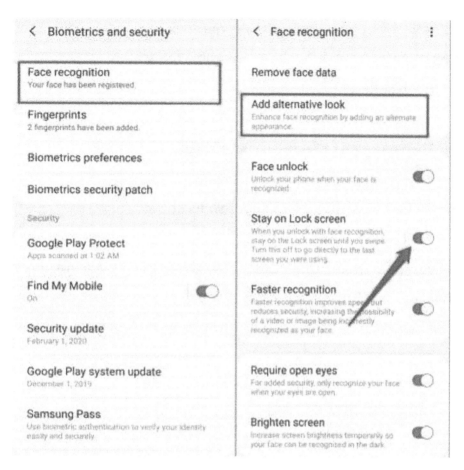

- Now run a dry test to confirm that it's working.

- You can also activate the 'Stay on Lock Screen' option on this same screen. This option configures your phone to remain on the lock screen after you unlock the phone. This will help prevent misdialing or accidental app launches when your phone opens accidentally.

Activate Lockdown Mode

You also have the option to lock down your device. If you are ever in a situation where you do not want people to have access to your phone, the button will automatically disable your device's fingerprint sensor and Iris scanner/ facial recognition. To enable this feature,

- Go to settings.
- Click on **Lock Screen.**
- Then navigate to **Secure Lock Settings.**
- Enter your password, pattern or pin.
- You will now see the option for **Show Lockdown.**
- Activate the **Lockdown Mode.**

You have now activated the Lockdown Mode. To use this feature, press and hold down the power button until you get some options displayed on your screen. Now click on **Lockdown** to secure your phone from third-party.

Note: once you activate the Lockdown mode, you have automatically turned off notifications, biometrics unlock, and smart lock on the Lock Screen.

Hide Sensitive Apps
Smartphones are not just to make calls and send messages as you can now do more with your smartphone. Some of the apps we use contain sensitive and personal information that we want to keep secret. The steps below will guide you on how to hide apps on your Note 20:

- Long-press on a blank space on the home screen.
- Then click on **Home Screen Settings.**
- Scroll down and click on **Hide Apps.**

- Choose the apps you want to hide and click on **Apply**

How to Unhide Apps
- Long-press on a blank space on the home screen
- Then click on **Home Screen Settings**
- Scroll down and click on **Hide Apps**
- Click on the minus (-) sign beside hidden apps at the top of your screen.
- Once done, click on **Apply.**

Secured Folder

This feature is used to protect specified emails, photos, contacts, or apps from third-party access. It serves as another layer of security. Follow the steps below to create your secure folder

- Go to **Settings.**
- Click on **Biometrics and Security.**
- Tap **Secure Folder.**

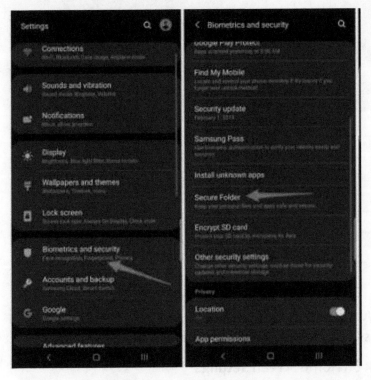

- Then follow the prompts to set up your secure folder successfully

Hide Sensitive Files with Secured Folder

We all have a sensitive file we do not want others to see, an odd photo we want to keep private or an app or game that we do not want another person to view on our phone. Samsung allows you to hide these files with the Secure Folder. Follow the steps below to use this feature

- Pull down the notification bar.
- Click on the **Secure Folder** icon.

- Agree to the terms and conditions then proceed to set up a Samsung account, if you don't have one already

- After signing in successfully, you will have a secure folder that you can only access with your fingerprint, pattern, password, or PIN.

- Proceed to add individual files and apps to the secure folder

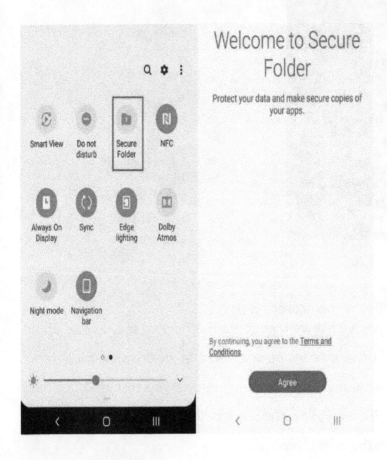

Hide The Secure Folder

Follow the steps below to hide the secure folder app:

- Go to **Settings.**

- Click on **Biometrics and Security.**

- Tap **Secure Folder.**

- Click on **Hide Secure Folder.** Then tap **OK.**

Access Files When the Secure Folder is Hidden
To access files in the hidden secure folder,

- Go to settings.

- Click on **Biometrics and Security.**

- Tap **Secure Folder.**

- Then click on the icon for the file you want to access at the bottom of the screen

Find My Mobile
Samsung has the 'Find My Mobile' service on all Galaxy devices. To access the setting,

- Go to the settings app.

- Click on **Biometrics and Security.**

- Then click on **Find My Mobile.**

- Feel free to adjust the settings to your preference.

- If you ever lose your phone, visit findmymobile.samsung.com, input your Samsung login details to access your Samsung account, and control or track down a lost phone.

Chapter 17: Manage Your Notification Settings

To quickly access your settings, notifications and more, open the notification panel

View the Notification panel
To access the notification panel from anywhere on your phone,

- Drag down the status bar to display the notification panel.

- Swipe further down to see your notification details.

- Click on an item to open it.

- Drag a notification to the right or left to clear a single notification.

- Click on the notification settings to customize notifications.

- Close the notification panel by clicking the Back key or dragging upward from the bottom of your screen.

Touch and Hold to See Notifications

You can change the way notifications are displayed on your device. To do this

- Go to the home screen and long-press on any blank part of the screen.
- Click on **Home Screen Settings.**
- Select **App icon badges.**
- Scroll down on the screen and move the switch beside **Show Notifications** to the right to enable.
- Once this feature is enabled, whenever you touch and hold down on an icon in the app drawer or on the home screen, unread notifications will show in a pop-up window for you to quickly check them without having to open the app

Snooze Alerts

The settings below will guide you on how to remove alerts from the notification shade for a defined period by snoozing them.

- Slowly swipe left or right on an alert until a bell and a settings icon appear.

- Click on the bell.

- Choose from the amount of time listed on the next screen to snooze the alert.

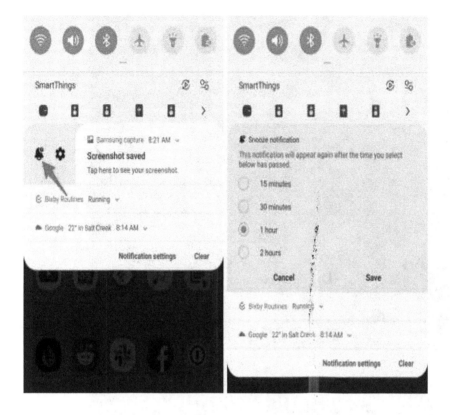

Set Notification Reminders

Are you aware that your phone can send you reminders to check missed notifications for specific apps? To activate this,

- Go to the settings app.

- Search for **Notification Reminder** in the search bar.

- Click on **Remind Every** and choose your preferred time interval.

- Then, navigate to **Selected Reminders** section and move the switch to the right for all the apps that you want.

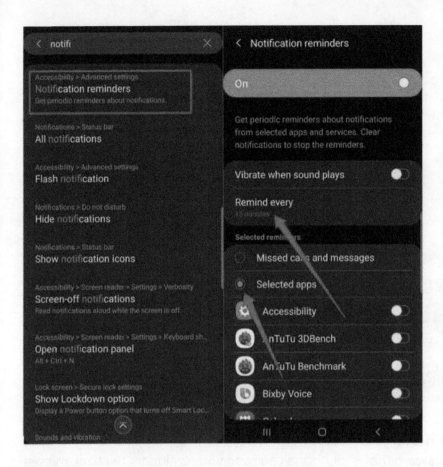

Enable Flashlight Notifications

This feature is particularly helpful when you are in a dark environment, movie theatre, or when your phone is in silent mode. This feature flashes the LED to notify you of incoming calls and messages.

- Go to settings.

- Click on **Accessibility.**

- Select **Advanced Settings.**

- Click on **Flashlight Notification.**

- Now toggle on the option for **Screen flash** and **Camera flash**

Direct access

Power and Volume up keys
Off

Volume up and down keys
Talkback

Notifications

Flash notification

Notification reminders
Get periodic reminders about notifications.

Direction lock
Unlock the screen by swiping in a series of directions.

Flash the camera light or the screen when you receive notifications or when alarms sound.

Camera flash

Screen flash

176

Enable Wi-Fi Calling on the Galaxy Note 20

Wi-fi calling uses your home Wi-fi network rather than your cell phone signals to make calls. This is mostly for times when the cellular signals are bad. The added bonus to this is that you get to enjoy higher call quality. This is how to enable it on your Note 20

- Go to settings.

- Click on **Connections.**

- Now toggle on the switch for **Wi-Fi calling.**

Enable Wifi Calling from the Note 20 Dialer

If you are unable to see the Wi-fi calling toggle under your phone settings, you can enable it directly from the phone dialer.

- Open the dialer from your home screen.

- Click on the overflow menu, that is, the three vertical dots ⋮ on the right — select **Settings.**

- Then toggle on **Wi-fi Calling.**

- You can now begin to enjoy the smoothness of Wi-fi calling

Using the Google Duo in the Phone Dialer
Samsung integrated the Google Duo directly into the dialer for the Note 20 series so that you can easily make video calls with family and friends. Here's a guide on how to make Duo calls

- Open the phone dialer.

- Choose the contact you want to video call.

- Click on the Duo icon under the contact's details to begin a video call.

- Your video call will now be transferred over to Duo.

- You can also move from a regular voice call to a video call. To do this while on a voice call, click on the video call button to switch to Duo video call.

Chapter 19: Maximizing Display on the Galaxy Note 20

Always On Display

This beautiful feature gives your phone a super chic look while displaying notifications, weather info, battery percentage, and time. You can also add stylish watch faces to display above it. To enable this feature,

- Go to Settings. Click on **Lock Screen.**

- Navigate to **Always On Display** and move the switch to the right to activate.

- You can customize it further by tapping on the card and selecting **Display Mode.** Then click on **Show Always.**

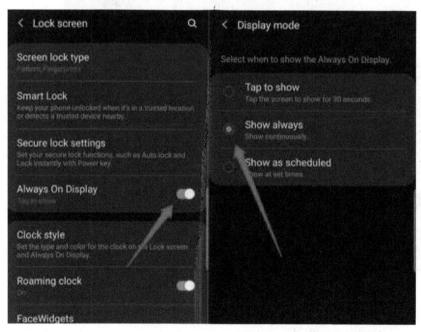

- Then return to the **Lock Screen** page and click on **Clock Style**

- Click on **Always-on Display,** and you will see various options to choose from.

- Pick the one you like and tap the **Done** button.

- Lock your phone and see the beautiful display come alive

Note: You can also change the color of the Clock Faces. To do this, simply click on **Color** under **Clock Style** and choose your preferred color.

Always on Display (AOD) Themes
Use custom themes for AOD.

- Go to the home screen and long-press on any blank part of the screen.

- Click on **Themes** . Select **AODs.**

- Click on an AOD to preview and download to **'My Always On Displays.'**

- To view all your downloaded AODs, click on **My Page** .

- Then choose the one you want to use and click on **Apply.**

Max Out the Display Resolution

The Note 20 display isn't automatically set at the maximum resolution in a bid to save battery life. But, setting your phone to the maximum resolution will help you enjoy some sharpness on your device.

- Go to the settings app. Click on **Display.**

- Select **Screen Resolution.**

- Choose your preferred resolution. The maximum is 3040 by 1440 pixels

Screen brightness

Adjust your screen brightness to suit your personal preferences or lighting condition.

- Go to settings. Click on **Display**

- On the next screen, drag the slider under **Brightness** to your desired settings

- Click on **Adaptive brightness** to automatically adjust the brightness of your screen based on the current lighting conditions

182

Enable Screen Zoom

This option is for people who like their screen bigger than the default size.

- Open the Settings app and tap **Display.**

- Tap **Screen Zoom,** then drag the slider to the left and to the right to set your preferred screen size.

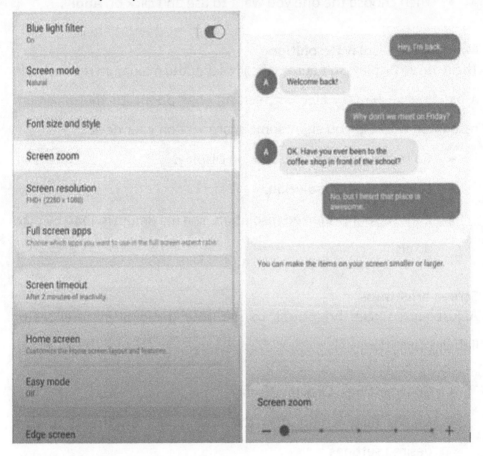

Change Refresh Rate

One of the major highlights of the newest additions to the Samsung family is the 120Hz refresh rate screen. This rate makes daily interactions to be smooth. By default, the refresh rate is set to 60Hz, but you can switch to 120Hz with the steps below

- Go to settings. Click on **Display** .

- Select **Motion smoothness.**

- Click on **Adaptive,** and your phone will automatically switch between the 120Hz and 60 Hz for Galaxy Note 20 Ultra.

- Then click on **Apply** to confirm the changes.

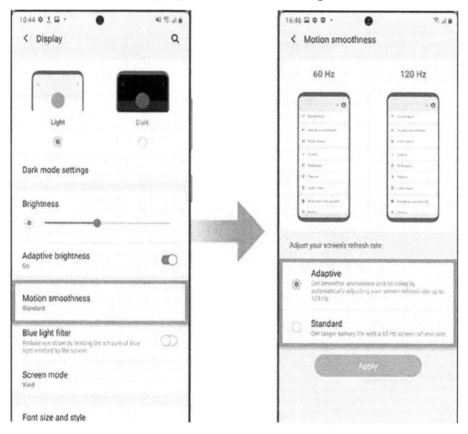

Note: the 120Hz mode uses up your battery faster because the screen is effectively refreshing twice as quickly as usual.

Screen mode

Your phone has several screen mode options that you can adjust to meet different situations for screen quality. Feel free to choose the mode that suits you.

- Go to settings. Click on **Display** .

- Click on **Screen Mode** and choose from the different screen modes displayed on your screen.

Blue light filter

This feature, particularly for those that operate their phone at night, helps you to sleep better. You can set up a schedule to automatically enable or disable this feature

- Go to settings. Click on **Display** .

- Click on **Blue light filter** and choose from the displayed option.

  1. Click **Turn On Now** to enable the feature.

  2. Pull the opacity slider to set the opacity of the filter.

  3. Click on **Turn on as scheduled** to create a schedule for when the feature should be enabled. You can choose either the **Custom schedule** or **Sunset to sunrise.**

Hide Front Camera

The NOTE 20 has its punch-hole camera in the top middle side of the screen, and it may become a bother when watching movies on the device. The good news is that you can hide the front camera. To do this

- Go to settings. Click on **Display.**

- Select **Full-Screen Apps**

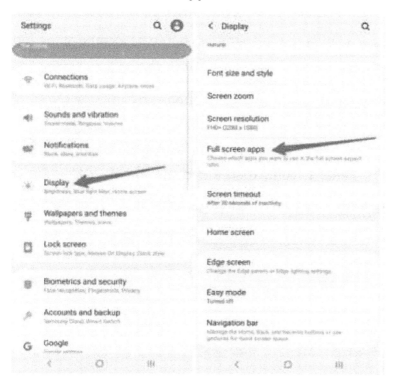

- Then toggle on the switch for **Hide Front Camera.**
- A little black bar will now appear at the top of your screen to cover the front camera

Show Brightness Bar on Top

To access the brightness bar, you need to swipe to the bottom of your screen. But you can configure the brightness bar to be located at the top of the notification bar.

- Swipe down to the bottom of your phone screen.

- Tap ⋮ by the top right side of your device screen.

- Tap **Quick Panel Layout,** then move the switch beside **Show Brightness on Top** to the right to enable it. Click on **Done** to complete.

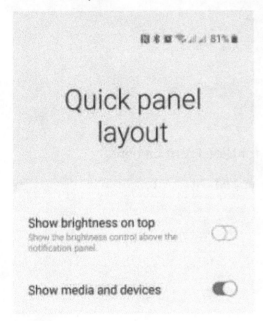

Customize Dark Mode

Dark mode switches your phone from a very bright interface to a dark theme on your phone's operating systems and apps. Not only does this mode help to save battery life, but it also eases the strain that bright light causes to the eyes. Here is how you can activate the option:

- Open the Setting app and tap **Display.**
- At the top part of your screen, select **Dark** to switch to Dark mode.

- Tap **Dark Mode Setting** to make changes and customize as you like.
- Move the switch beside **Turn on as Scheduled** to enable dark mode from sunset to sunrise automatically.
- If you want dark mode on your wallpaper, move the switch beside **Apply to Wallpaper** to the right to complete.

Switch to Vivid Display

The default display of the Note 20 has a natural look rather than the standard Vivid setting that Samsung users are familiar with. If you think the colors are not as intense as you prefer, you can switch to the Vivid display with the steps below

- Go to settings.

- Click on **Display.**

- Tap **Screen Mode.**

- Then click on **Vivid.**

- Move the slider to the left if you love a bluish hue.

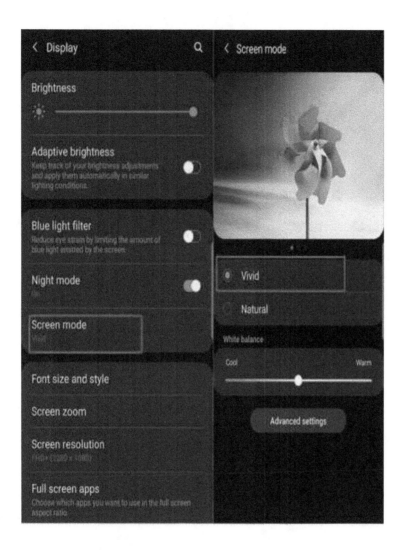

190

Chapter 20: Advanced Features of the Note 20

Dual Messenger

Most recent apps now have the Dual Messenger feature. This feature allows you to use more than one account of the same app like Snapchat or WhatsApp. To enable this feature,

- Go to settings. Click on **Advanced features.**

- Select **Dual Messenger** and toggle on the option for all the apps you want to clone.

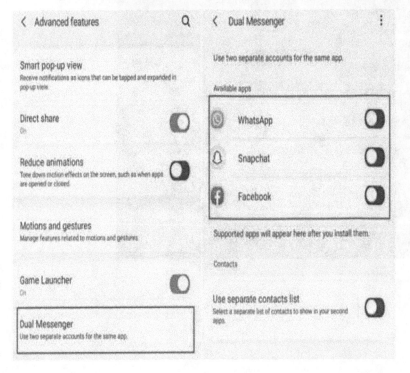

Get the Good Lock App

The Good Lock app from Samsung works well with the Note 20 series. The features of the app are easy to understand. The first one allows you to shrink the **Overview Selection menu** while the other one will enable you to view your notifications in a resizable window. To enjoy these features, you need first to install the Good lock app, after which you should install individual modules like the QuickStar and the Task Changer. After you download the app, you can use it to customize your lock screen as well as your one-hand operations.

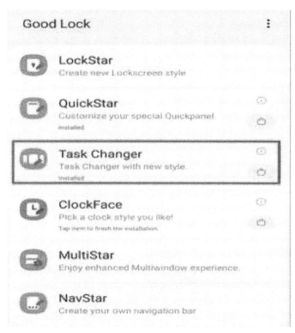

To activate the Mini mode,

- Open the Good lock app.
- Click on **Task Changer,** toggle on the option.
- Then toggle on the switch for Mini Mode.
- On the same screen, you may also want to explore the different layout types.

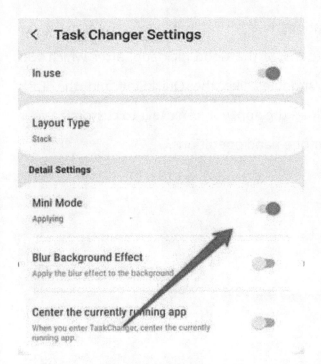

- Go back to the home screen of the app.
- Click on **QuickStar** and toggle on the option.
- Then enable the Notification Popup Button.

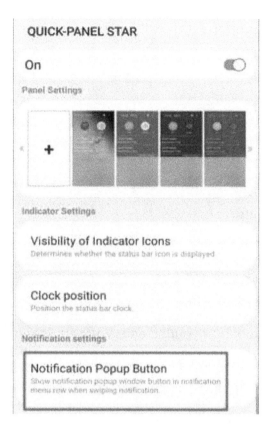

QUICK-PANEL STAR

On

Panel Settings

+

Indicator Settings

Visibility of Indicator Icons
Determines whether the status bar icon is displayed

Clock position
Position the status bar clock

Notification settings

Notification Popup Button
Show notification popup window button in notification
menu row when swiping notification.

- Once activated, you will see a button displayed in the notification bubble. Once you click on it, it will automatically open your notifications in a resizable window.

Samsung capture 11:41
Screenshot saved
Tap here to see your screenshot.

Note: Not all apps on your device supports this feature. Instagram does not support it, but Whatsapp does.

Assistant Menu

This feature is for persons that have motor control or other physical impairments. The Assistant menu allows you to access hardware buttons and other parts of the screen just by swiping or typing. Follow the steps below to activate this feature:

- Go to settings. Click on **Accessibility.**

- Then click on **Interaction and Dexterity.**

- Now enable the **Assistant Menu** option.

- The Assistant menu will appear on your screen. You can drag it to any part of the screen that you want.

- Click on the menu button to access options like the Screen off, back button, Volume, Home button, Screenshots, Recents button, and so on.

Screen reader
Get spoken audio guidance and special controls that help you
navigate without needing to see the screen.

Visibility enhancements
Change size, contrast, and colour to meet your needs.

Hearing enhancements
Adjust the audio to help your hearing, or use alternatives like text.

Interaction and dexterity
Enhance or replace touch interactions and other controls.

Advanced settings
Manage Direct access and other advanced functions

Installed services
1 service and 1 service

Universal switch
Control your phone with custom switches.

Assistant menu
Show a menu of easy-to-reach buttons that let you replace
hard key, gesture, and other common interactions

Click after pointer stops
Click automatically when the pointer stops moving

Interactions

Answering and ending calls

Interaction control
Block touch interaction for the Back, Home, and Recents
buttons, the keyboard, and a selected area of the screen.

Touch settings

Touch and hold delay
Short (0.5 seconds)

Pin Windows Feature

This feature means launching an app and pinning the app to your screen so that you do not accidentally close the app. Note that when an app is pinned, you will be unable to use other features outside the app, calls, and messages will also be blocked. To activate this feature,

- Go to settings. Click on **Biometrics and Security.**

- Select **Other Security Settings.**

- Then enable the option for **Pin Windows.**

Once you have enabled this feature, you can begin to pin any app. To pin an app,

- Launch the app as normal.

- Then press the recent app button.

- Click on the app icon located at the top of your screen.

- Then select **Pin this app.**

To close the pinned app

- Press and hold simmer down until you see the recent apps and back soft button.
- Click on it to close.

Using Pop-up View

This feature is a smart option that permits some specific apps to pop-up on top of other apps. This is similar to how Facebook Messenger operates. When this feature is active, any new message that comes into your phone comes as a round pop-up icon that you can click on to launch the messaging app. This feature can only be used with apps that support multi-window. To activate this feature

- Go to settings. Click on **Advanced Features.**
- Click on **Smart Pop-Up View.**
- Remember to toggle on only apps that support multi-window. However, this feature is best for messaging apps

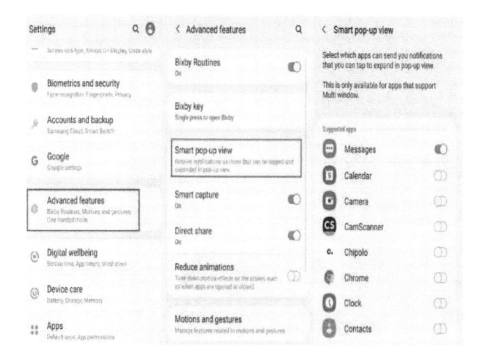

Split-screen apps

Your device allows you to use more than one app per time. To do this,

- Navigate to the multitasking view and look for any of the apps you want to access in the split-screen mode.

- Click on the app's icon.

- Then click on **Open in Split-Screen View.**

- The first app you launch will automatically minimize to the top of the screen until you launch the second app.

Enable One-Handed Mode

One of the first options you should enable on your phone is the conventional one-handed mode. With this option, you can either swipe up diagonally from the corners of the home screen or tap three times on the home screen to shrink the screen, thereby making it easy to work. This mode is most useful when typing or using your phone in a crowded environment. But you have to activate the feature manually using the steps below:

- Go to Finder and type 'one-handed' in the search bar.

- Click on the settings card, as shown in the screenshot below.
- Now toggle the switch for **One-handed Mode.**

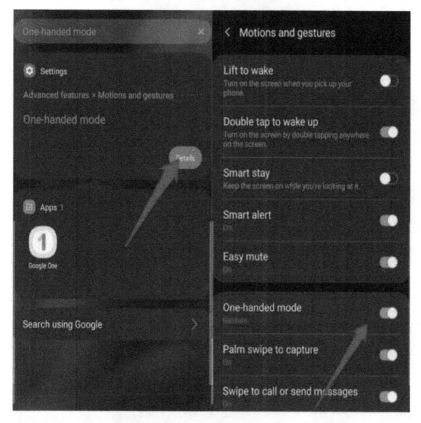

Another way to activate this feature is

- Go to settings.
- Click on **Motions and Gestures.**
- Now select between **Button** or **Gesture.**

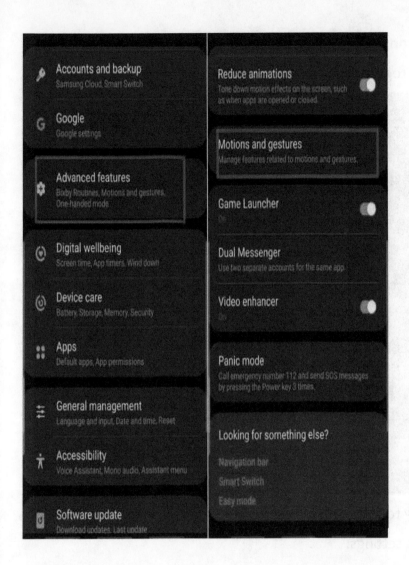

One-Hand Operation + App

This app was designed by Samsung to customize the navigation gestures further and is particularly useful for users who find it challenging to get to the bottom half of their device. It comes with two customizable handles on both sides of the device and allows you to perform functions like launching the previous app, going back, and opening recent menus just by swiping any of the handles. You can customize these handles to your taste. For now, each of the handles supports three gestures: horizontal, diagonal down, and diagonal up.

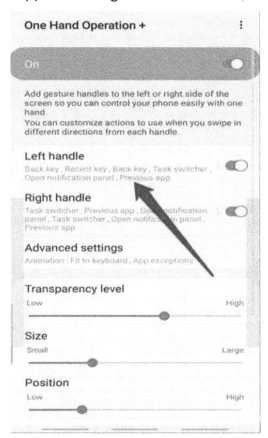

To set the gestures,

- Click on a handle and add your desired action
- You can also add Long Swipe gestures and then customize it

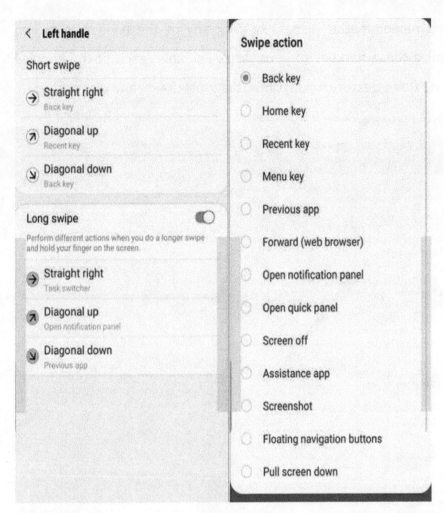

It may take some time for you to get used to these new gestures, but once you familiarize yourself with them, you will enjoy navigating the screen of your Note 20.

Cool tip: you can have the Edge screen on one edge and the One Hand Operation+ on the other edge, depending on your preference and convenience.